The Urban Dreamer Cookbook
Copyright © 2024 by Adrienne Evatt
All rights reserved.

No part of this book may be reproduced, distributed, or transmitted in any form or by any means, including photocopying, recording, or other electronic or mechanical methods, without the prior written permission of the publisher, except in the case of brief quotations embodied in critical reviews and certain other noncommercial uses permitted by copyright law. For permission requests, contact the publisher at the address below.

Published by Adrienne Evatt Coaching
Auburn, California, 95603 USA
AdrienneEvatt.com
UrbanDreamerFarm.org

Disclaimer:
The information provided in this book is for educational and informational purposes only. The author is not a licensed nutritionist, dietitian, or medical professional. Any advice regarding health and diet is intended as a general guide and should not be taken as medical advice. Always consult with a qualified healthcare provider before making changes to your diet or lifestyle.

ISBN: 978-1-965886-01-4
Printed in the United States of America
First Edition, 2024

CONTENTS

Introduction 06

Shopping 10

Chapter One Good Morning 14

Chapter Two Pastas & Sauces 36

Chapter Three Meals You Always Want 58

Chapter Four Sides & Salads 96

Chapter Five Fancy Pants 120

Chapter Six Sweets Upon Sweets 154

Chapter Seven Adrienne's Afterthoughts 196

Index 224

Acknowledgments 233

Letter from the Author 235

The Story & Dedication 236

Other Books by Adrienne 245

Your Review 246

The URBAN Dreamer COOKBOOK

Comfort Foods That Feel Like Home
Flavors that Evoke Love, Warmth,
and Unforgettable Memories

ADRIENNE EVATT

Introduction

ur·ban
/ˈərbən/
adjective
1. in, relating to, or characteristic of a town or city.
"the urban population"

dream·er
/ˈdrēmər/
noun
noun: dreamer; plural noun: dreamers
1. a person who dreams or is dreaming.
a person who is unpractical or idealistic.

URBAN Dreamer started in Los Angeles, California.

Hi, I'm Adrienne Evatt and I started URBAN Dreamer in 2012 when I was pregnant with my second child. My family and I lived in Los Angeles, California with our dogs and a small front and backyard. While we were in the city limits, we did live in a cute little neighborhood near the international airport (LAX) and the beach (ooh la la). In our little front yard, we had a white picket fence, where I grew seasonal fruits and vegetables in the beds in front of and inside the fence. We had avocado and apricot trees in the front yard. We had a tomato garden, multi stone-fruit tree (fruit salad tree) a micro vineyard and a small garden and chicken coop. I started a blog called Urban Dreamer that had various articles on cooking, gardening and homesteading in an urban setting. While working full-time as a corporate executive, I continued my blog and expanded to a small Farmstand on weekends. Our top sellers were Fig Pecan Jam with Port (page 203) and Magic Spaghetti Sauce (page 46).

Several years later, we relocated to a Northern California 20-acre farm. Once we were a little settled, I left my corporate career, and we started a small Farmstand. We thought it only fitting to name the new farm, The Urban Dreamer Farms and Vineyard, so we kept our name, and we did!

The Farmstand started with a smattering of garden starts, fresh eggs, muffins, jams and crispy granola. I kept coming back, week after week, and grew and grew and grew. I leaned into the products that were the most popular, and it was not our incredible farm fresh produce... to my surprise it was my baked goods. So, more and more baked goods were offered, and we expanded from muffins and granola to pies, cakes, breads, enchiladas, soups, salad, salsa, guacamole, casseroles and more. I LOVED it. I was in the kitchen cooking, creating recipes and gardening and the family was enjoying the joys and trials of farm life.

As the Farmstand grew, there were so many customers who asked me to create a cookbook. What they didn't know was that I had been working on a book of family recipes for over 20 years, and that many of those recipes were the Farmstand favorites.

My parents and my own travel were the biggest influences to my cooking, although for very different attributes.

Dad was a world traveling businessman who never said no to trying new things (there's a story about that later in the book). He especially loved refined and fancy cuisine, but also appreciated the very best of absolutely anything, including enchiladas, breakfast and pie. He instilled in me a pursuit of perfection and always striving to make everything better, more special and more unique. But what came out of that also were some magically tender food memories, laced with emotions from joyful times, family events, and special family affairs. What is more incredible than a food memory? Just a taste and you can be completely transported, including tastes, smells, swelling hearts and sounds of laughter and singing. Many say that food memories are the strongest, and I agree wholeheartedly.

Mom was a master of math and efficiency. These were hallmarks of her personality. So, while she did most of the cooking growing up, she was a MASTER of finding time savers, shortcuts and simplifications. She challenged every assumption in a recipe, and constantly attempted new ways to improve the PROCESS of making a recipe. Because of her, I am always challenging the way to make things and finding better and faster ways to make food great.

My many years as a corporate executive included massive amounts of global travel. From Kansas City, Kansas and Bangor, Maine to Tokyo, Japan and Florence, Italy. I ate my way through my travels. Tasting so may new global foods opened my eyes to taste explosions, and any time I found something I loved, I tried to figure out how it could have been made. Sometimes I would guess and ask the chef. I watched the Food Network and paid attention to how chefs made things and why. I studied cookbooks by Americas Test Kitchen which explain the science behind each set of recipe attempts in great detail. When I was home, I cooked. A LOT.

So the food in this book is a collection of global travel, local favorites, and family memories. It spans fancy dinners and quickie salads, as well as luscious pie (Nectarine Pie, page 158) and the BEST Lasagne Bolognese (page 48). This is somewhat of a teaching book, as I thrive on sharing all of my cool tricks and discoveries. Some recipes are quick and some a bit more advanced, but ALL are comfort foods. They are meant to invite you into your own kitchen, bring you the joy of creating something delicious and wonderful, and the magic of creating your own powerful memories. Happy cooking! It's going to be so good!

Smart Grocery Shopping

Shopping for a Well-Stocked Kitchen

When planning meals, the key to success begins long before you enter the kitchen—it starts at the grocery store (or at your local farm). Shopping strategically not only saves time and money but also ensures you have all the ingredients necessary to create delicious, balanced meals. This chapter will guide you through the essentials of shopping for fresh produce, bread, cheeses, dairy, and shelf-stable goods, as well as how to plan and stock your pantry with unique ingredients that will elevate your cooking. Plus, you'll learn how having a well-stocked pantry and refrigerator can simplify your life and enhance your creativity in the kitchen.

1. Planning Ahead: Crafting a Grocery List

Before heading to the store, it's helpful to plan out your meals for the week. Consider the recipes you want to make, the variety of foods you'll need, and how to balance your meals with proteins, vegetables, and grains. Planning not only prevents food waste but also ensures you'll have everything you need for a quick, stress-free week of cooking.

2. Shopping for Fresh Fruits and Vegetables

When buying produce, quality matters. Here's what to look for to ensure you're getting the freshest fruits and vegetables:

- **Fruits**: Look for bright, vibrant colors, which often indicate ripeness and freshness. Check for firmness in apples, pears, and grapes; they should feel dense and firm. Bananas, berries, and citrus fruits should have a pleasant, sweet fragrance. Avoid fruits with soft spots, blemishes, or mold. For seasonal fruits like peaches or plums, they should give slightly when pressed gently. Cantaloupe should smell sweet at the stem end.

- **Vegetables**: Choose vegetables that are crisp and free of wilting or browning. Leafy greens like spinach or kale should be dark green and perky, not slimy or yellowing. Root vegetables like carrots, potatoes, and onions should feel firm and free of sprouts or cracks. For items like tomatoes, avocados, or peppers, a gentle squeeze should give you an idea of ripeness—slightly soft means they are ready to eat.

- **Seasonal Buying**: Whenever possible, purchase fruits and vegetables that are in season. They'll be fresher, more flavorful, and often more affordable. Consider visiting a local farmer's market for in-season produce that may not be available at the grocery store.

3. Bread: Fresh vs. Shelf-Stable

Bread can be one of the most versatile staples in your kitchen. When choosing bread, consider your week's needs:

- **Fresh bread**: Look for crusty artisanal breads, sourdough, or whole-grain varieties at the bakery section. Fresh bread often contains fewer preservatives but has a shorter shelf life, so plan to use it within a few days.

- **Shelf-stable bread**: Packaged bread, such as sandwich loaves or pita bread, is great for long-term storage. Opt for whole grain or sprouted varieties, which offer more nutrients and fiber. And keeping them refrigerated or frozen will extend their usefulness.

4. Cheese and Dairy: Quality over Quantity

A well-rounded fridge isn't complete without a selection of cheeses and dairy products. Here's what to consider:

- **Cheeses**: When shopping for cheese, aim for quality over quantity. A few good-quality cheeses, like a sharp cheddar, creamy Brie, or tangy goat cheese, can go a long way. For everyday use, have a block of mozzarella or Parmesan on hand for easy grating. When purchasing cheese, opt for whole blocks over pre-shredded varieties, which can contain preservatives.

- **Dairy**: Look for high-quality dairy products like organic milk, sour cream, yogurt, and butter. Full-fat versions often offer better flavor and a more satisfying texture, plus they can be used sparingly. Greek yogurt is a great multi-use ingredient—perfect for breakfasts, snacks, or as a base for sauces and dressings.

5. Shelf-Stable Goods: Pantry Essentials and Unique Ingredients

Having a well-stocked pantry makes it easier to pull together a meal on short notice. Here are the essentials and some unique ingredients that can add flair to your cooking:

- **Pantry staples**: Keep basic ingredients on hand like rice, pasta, flour, sugar, beans, and canned tomatoes. These are the building blocks for countless meals, from soups and stews to pasta dishes and casseroles.

- **Unique ingredients**: To elevate your cooking, consider adding a few unique pantry items:

- **Smoked paprika**: Adds a rich, smoky depth to meats, stews, salsa, or roasted vegetables.
- **Harissa paste**: A spicy, flavorful North African condiment perfect for marinades, sauces, or dips.
- **Tahini**: A sesame paste often used in Middle Eastern cooking, great for making hummus or salad dressing.
- **Coconut milk**: Ideal for curries, soups, drinks, or even baking, adding a creamy, subtle sweetness.
- **Miso paste**: A fermented soybean paste that provides umami richness to soups, dressings, and marinades.
- **Canned fish**: Smoked trout, sardines,

mackerel, smoked oysters, or tuna can add a quick protein boost to salads, pastas, or sandwiches.
- **Dried mushrooms**: Porcini or shiitake mushrooms can add a savory depth to broths and sauces.
- **Unique vinegar**: Banyuls Vinegar or White Balsamic Vinegar can make a vinaigrette over-the-top amazing

6. Benefits of a Well-Stocked Pantry and Refrigerator

Having a well-stocked pantry and refrigerator allows you to cook spontaneously, avoid last-minute grocery runs, and make use of leftovers in creative ways. It also enables you to maintain a balance between healthy meals and indulgent treats, making your kitchen a versatile space for both everyday cooking and special occasions. With essential ingredients at your fingertips, you'll find it easier to create meals that are both delicious and nutritious, while also saving time and reducing stress.

Tips for Keeping Your Pantry Stocked:

- Regularly check expiration dates and rotate stock to ensure nothing goes to waste.

- Keep a list of pantry essentials and update it after each grocery trip.

- Invest in good storage containers to keep ingredients like flour, grains, and spices fresh longer.

By shopping wisely and maintaining a well-organized pantry and refrigerator, you'll set yourself up for culinary success. Your kitchen will be ready for anything—from quick weeknight meals to impressive dinner parties. With the right ingredients on hand, you can explore new recipes, stay flexible, and most importantly, enjoy the process of cooking.

Chapter One

Good Morning

There is something cozy and truly special about the morning sun as it greets you while eating breakfast. The smells, sights and sounds make it extra memorable. For me, it's the sound of grinding fresh espresso beans and the smell of coffee. It's also the humming sizzle and smell of bacon cooking. And the way warm maple syrup swirls and melts into butter on top of a steaming hot Apple Dutch Baby fills my soul. What a great way to begin a day!

"You have such deep wisdom"

-ADRIENNE EVATT

Good Morning

1. Granola 18
2. Challah 21
3. Zucchini Bread Cupcakes 23
4. Apple Dutch Baby 25
5. Berry Bran Muffins 26
6. Breakfast Cupcakes 29
7. Scones 31
8. Apple Cider Donut Cupcakes 32
9. Warm & Satisfying Eggnog 33
10. Roasted Asparagus with Soft Cooked Eggs 35

Granola

When Urban Dreamer Farm & Vineyard had our first farmstand in early 2018, this very granola made its debut. The high proportion of nuts and seeds vs. oatmeal makes this granola particularly high in vitamins, fiber, omega 3's, good fats and protein. It's slightly sweet, crunchy and delicious!

Makes 2 Quarts

- 4 cups *Bob's Red Mill* traditional organic rolled oats
- 1 cup mixed fancy nuts
- ½ cup macadamia nuts
- ½ cup pistachio nuts
- ½ cup pumpkin seeds (pepitas)
- 2 teaspoons chia seeds
- ½ teaspoon garam masala
- ½ teaspoon cinnamon
- ½ cup maple syrup
- 2 tablespoons brown sugar
- 2 tablespoons vegetable oil (or oil of your preference, like avocado, grapeseed, canola or even melted coconut oil)
- 1 cup dried fruit - I use a combination of dried blueberries and dried tart cherries or dried cranberries | craisins and apricots.

1. Preheat the oven to 350 degrees.
2. Line a cookie sheet with parchment paper and spray with cooking spray.
3. Mix oats, nuts and seeds in a large bowl.
4. Mix spices, maple syrup, brown sugar and vegetable oil in a large measuring cup until blended.
5. Add syrup mixture into oatmeal mixture until well-coated.
6. Pour onto the cookie sheet and bake for 20-25 minutes until lightly golden.

NOTE:

Don't stir the granola until it is completely cooled so you don't miss out on all those yummy clusters.

✏️ NOTE:

This bread recipe is also used to make cinnamon pecan twists, mini chocolate chip loaves and pinwheel style buns stuffed with ham, cheese and topped with poppy seeds. Creativity is your friend here. For smaller buns and twists, reduce the cooking time.

Challah Bread

This bread is so pretty, I love to give it as a gift! Braids of eggy, slightly sweet, soft Challah are the stuff of bread dreams. Enjoy this bread straight out of the oven, toasted with butter, as French toast or even as croutons.

Makes 1 Large Loaf

- 3 cups flour
- 1 teaspoon kosher salt
- 1 tablespoon yeast
- 3 tablespoons honey
- 3 eggs, one separated
- ½ cup room temperature water
- ¼ cup melted butter
- 1 tsp vegetable oil

1. Pour the teaspoon of vegetable oil into a glass, 2.5 quart or larger bowl and swirl it around.
2. In a mixer with a dough hook, Put the flour, salt, yeast and honey. Add 2 eggs, 1 egg yolk, water and melted butter. Save the egg white, mixed with a tablespoon of water, in the refrigerator for later.
3. Mix for about 2-5 minutes, until the dough looks like a smooth ball. If it looks wet and is not forming a ball, add flour a tablespoon at a time until it balls up. If it looks dry, add water a tablespoon at a time until it smooths out.
4. Dump the dough ball into the prepared bowl. Flip it over, and cover with plastic wrap. Leave in an undisturbed location for 2 hours so it can rise. The counter or an empty (turned off) oven are good spots.
5. After the 2 hours have passed, punch the dough ball down, flip it over, re-cover with plastic wrap and let rise another 45 minutes.
6. Preheat the oven to 375 degrees. Line a cookie sheet with parchment paper and spray with cooking spray.
7. Dump your dough onto a floured surface. Cut off one third of the dough. Cut both remaining pieces of dough (the 1/3 chunk and the 2/3 chunk) each, into thirds and braid them.
8. Place the larger braid on the cookie sheet and brush with reserved egg white mixture. Top with smaller braid and then brush the whole loaf with reserved egg white mixture again.
9. Let the braided dough sit for about 15 minutes and then bake for 25-35 minutes or until deeply golden and puffed.

Zucchini Bread Cupcakes

My summer squash harvest is always bountiful. In order to not waste a single bit of the harvest, I shred, measure and freeze zucchini for use throughout the year. Mostly to make this deliciously sweet and moist zucchini bread, baked up like little cupcakes.

Serves 36

- 6 cups flour
- 2 teaspoon salt
- 2 teaspoons baking soda
- 2 teaspoons baking powder
- 1 heaping tablespoon cinnamon
- 6 eggs
- 2 cups vegetable oil
- 4 ½ cups white sugar
- 2 tablespoons vanilla
- 4 cups grated zucchini

1. Preheat the oven to 325 degrees. Line a muffin tin with cupcake paper and spray with cooking spray.
2. Sift flour, salt, baking powder, baking soda and cinnamon together in a medium bowl.
3. Beat eggs, oil, vanilla and sugar together in a large bowl.
4. Add sifted ingredients to the creamed mixture and beat well. Stir in zucchini until well combined.
5. Fill muffin liners with 1 large scoop. Bake for 20-25 minutes.
6. Remove them from the oven and immediately sprinkle with a tablespoon of sugar.

NOTE:

These can also be made with yellow squash or other summer squash with equal affection. Use what you have!

Apple Dutch Baby

One of my absolute favorites! A big, puffy, buttery, delicate, eggy, slightly dense and a little sweet pancake that gets started on the stove and finishes cooking in the oven. It is gloriously dramatic when presented straight from the oven and it tastes absolutely wonderful. This is a Dutch baby!

Serves 4-5

- 1 cup flour
- 1 cup milk
- 4 eggs
- ¼ teaspoon kosher salt
- 1 crisp and slightly tart apple such as a Macoun, Pink Lady, Fuji or Honeycrisp
- 1 heaping tablespoon brown sugar
- 6 tablespoons butter (¾ of a stick)

1. Preheat the oven to 425 degrees. Slice the apple and cook with the butter and brown sugar at medium to medium-high heat in an ovenproof skillet until the apples soften. A cast iron skillet is great for this recipe, but any oven skillet will work if it can accommodate 425 degrees.

2. Meanwhile, put the flour, milk, eggs and salt in the blender and blend very well.

3. Once the apples have softened, pour the ingredients of the blender into the skillet and continue to let cook for about a minute or 2, just until you see the edges start to firm up.

4. Put the skillet in the lower third of the oven and cook for 15 minutes. Without opening the oven, reduce the heat to 350 and cook for another 10-15 minutes, until the pancake is puffy and golden.

5. Take it out of the oven and show it off to your friends. It's impressive! Serve immediately – I usually pop the whole thing out of the pan onto a big cutting board and slice it like a pizza. It's lovely just the way it is, as well as sprinkled with a little powdered sugar, or topped with maple syrup.

NOTE:

Modify this recipe by swirling 4 tablespoons of berry jam into it, halfway through the baking. You can also use a peach or nectarine instead of the apple, or just make it plain.

Berry Bran Muffins

These are not your everyday boring bran muffin! These bran muffins are moist, filling, delicious and substantial enough for breakfast, a snack or even dessert.

Serves 12

- 1 cup flour
- 1 teaspoon salt
- ½ teaspoon cinnamon
- ½ teaspoon baking soda
- ½ teaspoon baking powder
- 1 cup yogurt
- 1 cup brown sugar
- 2 eggs
- ½ cup vegetable oil
- 1 teaspoon vanilla
- 2 cups berries (blackberries, raspberries, chopped strawberries, or blueberries)
- 1 ½ cups wheat bran
- 1 cup wheat germ

1. Preheat the oven to 350 degrees. Line a 12-cup muffin tin with cupcake paper and spray with cooking spray.
2. Whisk the flour, salt, cinnamon, baking powder and baking soda in a large bowl.
3. In a separate bowl mix yogurt, brown sugar, eggs, oil and vanilla until completely blended.
4. Pour the yogurt and egg mixture into the flour mixture and stir gently until just blended and no streaks of flour remain.
5. Add the berries, wheat bran and wheat germ. Fold very lightly until mixed. At this point, the mixture can be covered and refrigerated overnight for cooking the next day.
6. Spoon the batter into the muffin pan and bake for 25-30 minutes or until a toothpick inserted into the center barely comes out clean.

NOTE:

Using loose frozen berries for this recipe is best. Modify with peaches and pecans, chocolate chips or replace the berries with a diced apple and an extra ½ teaspoon of cinnamon.

Breakfast Cupcakes

The Urban Dreamer breakfast cupcake is a farm stand favorite! It is high in protein and characterized by banana, peanut butter and chocolate. These delightful morsels are very moist, and delicious. The perfect breakfast sweet!

Serves 12

- 1 ½ cups flour
- ¾ cups sugar
- 1 ½ teaspoons baking powder
- ½ teaspoon salt
- 8 tablespoons (one stick) butter
- 2 bananas
- 1/3 cup crunchy or creamy peanut butter or other nut butter of choice or ½ cup canned pumpkin.
- ½ cup chocolate chips, plus 2 tablespoons for garnish
- ½ cup roasted pumpkin seeds, plus 2 tablespoons for garnish
- 2 tablespoons plain yogurt
- 1 large egg +2 large egg yolks at room temperature
- 1 ½ teaspoons vanilla extract

1. Preheat the oven to 350 degrees. Line a 12-cup muffin tin with cupcake paper and spray with cooking spray.
2. Mix flour, salt, sugar, baking powder, chocolate chips, and pumpkin seeds in a medium bowl. Set aside
3. In a large measuring cup (Pyrex 4 cups or other microwave proof cup), microwave 2 peeled whole bananas, covered with plastic wrap, for 2 ½ to 3 ½ minutes or until completely mushed / collapsed and liquid looking.
4. Carefully peel back the plastic wrap, mush with a fork and mix in the butter and peanut butter until melted. Let cool.
5. In a separate bowl, mix eggs, yogurt and vanilla with a fork until just combined.
6. Combine flour mixture, egg mixture, and cooled banana mixture until just mixed.
7. Fill cupcake liners with batter. Sprinkle the extra chocolate chips and pumpkin seeds on top.
8. Bake at 350° for 25 minutes or until a toothpick inserted into the center barely comes out clean. Remove from the oven and sprinkle with 1-2 tablespoons sugar.

✎ NOTE:

To reduce the sweetness, remove the chocolate chips or replace with ½ cup of blueberries.

✎ NOTE:

To make plain scones, omit the blueberries. For cranberry orange scones, replace the blueberries with dried cranberries and add 1 tablespoon orange zest and use orange juice in place of the milk for brushing on the tops

Blueberry Scones

I don't know anyone that doesn't love scones! Make and bake these right before you plan to eat and serve them. They are wonderfully delicious, rich and slightly sweet. Enjoy them fresh, served with clotted cream or whole butter and jam.

Serves 8

- 2 cups sifted all-purpose flour
- ¼ cup sugar, plus additional for sprinkling over tops
- 2 teaspoons baking powder
- ½ teaspoon salt
- 4 tablespoons cold, salted butter, cut into pieces
- 1/3 cup dried blueberries
- ½ cup whole milk
- 1 egg
- 2 tablespoons milk
- 2 tablespoons sugar

1. Preheat the oven to 425 degrees. Mix the flour, ¼ cup sugar, baking powder and salt in a large bowl.

2. Cover the dried blueberries with hot or boiling water and let sit for 10 minutes to plump, then drain.

3. Cut the butter into the flour mixture using 2 butter knives, a pastry blender or your fingers. Add blueberries.

4. Whisk together ½ cup milk and 1 egg. Pour into the flour mixture and mix with a fork until barely blended. The dough will be very moist and sticky.

5. Turn dough out onto lightly floured surface; gently knead 1 or 2 times to incorporate loose pieces of dough. **Do not over knead.**

6. Pat dough to 1 ½ inch thickness into a circle (about 9 inches across). Using a pizza cutter or very sharp knife, cut like a pizza into eight slices.

7. Place triangles onto lightly greased baking sheets. Brush the tops of the scones with an additional 2 tablespoons milk. Sprinkle with an additional 2 tablespoons sugar.

8. Bake until golden brown, about 14 to 17 minutes, rotating pan halfway through baking for more even browning. Promptly remove when they barely begin to turn golden on the edges.

9. Serve with clotted butter and jam!

Apple Cider Donut Cupcakes

Fall in Northern California means apple season! These cupcakes are reminiscent of those fresh, slightly crisp on the outside, pillowy soft and warm on the inside, apple cider donuts of your childhood, dusted when fresh out the deep fryer with cinnamon sugar.

Serves 26

- 6 cups flour
- 1 tablespoon baking powder
- 1 tablespoon cinnamon
- 1 teaspoon baking soda
- 1 ½ teaspoons salt
- 3 ½ cups sugar
- ½ cup apple cider or apple juice
- 3 cups applesauce
- 1 ½ cups olive oil
- 4 teaspoons vanilla
- 7 large eggs

Topping

- 4 tablespoons butter, melted
- ¼ cup sugar
- ½ teaspoon cinnamon

1. Preheat the oven to 350 degrees. Line a muffin tin with cupcake paper and spray with cooking spray.
2. In a large bowl, whisk together flour, baking powder, 1 tablespoon cinnamon, baking soda, and salt.
3. In another bowl, whisk together 1 ½ cups sugar, oil, applesauce, vanilla and eggs.
4. Add egg mixture to flour mixture; whisk until combined. Transfer to a prepared muffin pan, placing one large scoop into each muffin paper.
5. Bake for 20-25 minutes, rotating halfway through or until a toothpick inserted into the center barely comes out clean
6. Place the pan on a wire rack and let cool for 10 mins.
7. Meanwhile, mix the remaining ¼ cup sugar and ½ teaspoon cinnamon. Brush warm cupcakes with melted butter, then sprinkle liberally with cinnamon sugar. Let cool completely.

Warm & Satisfying Eggnog

I have gone through many phases of different eating programs. While nursing, I discovered that two of my daughters had infant food allergies. After which, I followed a very restricted diet until nursing was complete. During this time, I created some inspired recipes that also happen to be appealing to others on longer term restricted diets. This is one of them, a warm, rich and satisfying drink that is loaded with minerals, vitamins, nutrition and protein.

Serves 1

- 3 farm fresh eggs
- 1 tablespoon peanut butter powder or almond butter or 2 tablespoons raw cashews
- ½ to 1 scoop vanilla protein powder
- pinch of salt
- ¼ teaspoon cinnamon
- 1 tablespoon butter
- 2 tablespoons collagen hydrolysate powder
- sweetener of choice – sugar, honey, stevia, coconut sugar, agave, maple syrup (optional)
- 2 ½ cups boiling water
- 1 espresso (optional)

1. Add all the ingredients to your blender except the boiling water and espresso.
2. Start the blender and slowly add the boiling water and espresso.
3. Blend for 20-30 seconds, or until blended. Enjoy!

✎ NOTE:

To remove the foam, pour into a gravy boat/fat separator. Let sit for 1 minute then pour into your cup.

Roasted Asparagus with Soft Cooked Eggs

I must say, there is something amazing about the pairing of cooked asparagus and eggs. In Paris, it is common to see them everywhere. Plates with roasted asparagus and scrambled eggs, roasted asparagus and hollandaise sauce, roasted asparagus and soft, cooked eggs, made extra fancy with a drop of truffle oil. Just divine! Here is my take on roasted asparagus and soft, cooked eggs. This is one of my favorite brunches, topped with a little shaved pecorino cheese and maybe even a little pile of sliced prosciutto or Serrano ham.

Serves 3-6

- 2 pounds asparagus, rinsed and woody stems broken off the bottom
- olive oil
- salt and pepper
- 6 cold eggs
- freshly grated parmigiano or pecorino cheese

1. Preheat the oven to 400 degrees.
2. Place asparagus on a large cookie sheet, one layer thick.
3. Drizzle with olive oil and then sprinkle with salt and pepper.
4. Cook in the top third of the oven at 400 degrees for 5-15 minutes, depending on the thickness of your asparagus. It should still be slightly firm, and the ends should have a little bit of toasty looking edges.
5. Remove from the oven and let cool slightly.
6. Meanwhile, heat about a ½ inch of water to boiling in a saucepan with a lid.
7. Place the cold eggs in the pan and cook (it steams them) for 6 ½ minutes.
8. Rinse with cold water for one minute, and then peel the eggs.
9. Serve immediately by placing a few asparagus spears on each plate, an egg or 2 cut in half on top and then season the whole thing with salt, freshly ground pepper, and freshly grated cheese (parmesan or pecorino) to taste. Enjoy!

Chapter Two

Pastas & Sauces

What's more comforting than a nice bowl of pasta with a velvety unctuous sauce. Regardless of the season, plain or buttered, fresh or boxed pasta, I love the texture of pasta. The flavor and even the scent is so inviting. Let's tuck into a nice big bowl.

"Consider the fact that you are extraordinary."

-ADRIENNE EVATT

Pastas & Sauces

1. Fresh Pasta 40
2. Oven Roasted Spaghetti Sauce 43
3. Sicilian Spaghetti Sauce 45
4. Even Better, BEST Spaghetti Sauce 46
5. Bolognese Sauce & Lasagna Bolognese 48
6. Broccoli Bacon Carbonara 52
7. Pasta with Brussels Sprouts 55
8. Ribollita 56

Fresh Pasta

My 2 favorite things to make with my egg bounty are fresh pasta and custard. In my early twenties I traveled to Florence, Italy and it was there that I discovered the most amazing pasta ever, made with eggs. I came home to raise my own hens and learn the craft of pasta making. It's a messy delight to make fresh pasta with my daughters and it is so wonderfully delicious.

Yield - 2 pounds

- 4 cups flour
- 3 large eggs
- 6 egg yolks from large eggs
- 4 tablespoons olive oil
- 1/3 cup water + ice

1. Put the flour in the food processor and process for a few seconds. Mix all remaining ingredients in a large measuring cup.

2. Turn the food processor on, and slowly pour liquids in with the machine running. It should come together in a ball in 30-45 seconds. If it looks wet and sticky, add a little flour. If it looks dry and crumbly and does not form a ball, add a little more ice water.

3. Lightly coat the ball of pasta in flour. Lightly sprinkle inside a zip top bag or sheet of plastic wrap with flour. Wrap the pasta ball in the plastic and put it in the freezer or on the counter, depending on when you want to finish making the pasta. I typically put a pound in the fridge and a pound in the freezer.

4. The dough ball needs to come back to room temp and rest for about 30-60 minutes before you roll it out.

5. Cut each one-pound ball of pasta into 4 pieces.

6. Roll each piece through the pasta machine one at a time. Keep the pasta lightly floured and begin with the thickest setting on your machine. Once the dough has become a sort of sheet, fold it into 3rd's. Turn it 45 degrees and send it through the roller again. Do this twice, and it will work to knead your dough and make the edges of the pasta smooth and uniform

7. Continue rolling each piece working towards a thinner setting, or the setting that works for the type of pasta you desire. Flour each section between rolling and cutting to keep it from getting sticky. Store in the refrigerator to keep it cool between each use.

8. Cut each sheet of pasta crosswise into 2 or 3 pieces so they are shorter. Then cut by hand, or use a pasta cutting attachment, into the shape and thickness that you want. For Fettuccine use a wide flat noodle. Pappardelle is a double wide fettuccine noodle. Maltagliati are randomly shaped pieces. Bow ties are made from little squares, or other small shapes as desired.

9. Shake off any excess flour. Bring a large pot of salted boiling water to a rolling boil.

10. Cook noodles for 1-2 minutes stirring to avoid clumping. Taste a small piece to make sure it is cooked to your liking.

NOTE:

Spread pasta out on a cookie sheet or board and freeze. Store in an airtight container or plastic freezer bag. Cook frozen pasta the same as your fresh pasta, just give it a little more time to cook.

Oven Roasted Spaghetti Sauce

I think tomatoes from a home garden in late summer are biblically good. Like crazy, sweet, juicy, amazing, good. There are a few favorite things I like to do with those unique summer tomatoes. One of my favorites is oven-roasted tomato sauce. When you have pounds and pounds of fresh tomatoes it's nice to be able to preserve that glorious summer flavor in the freezer for a midwinter treat.

Makes 2 Quarts

- 20 cups garden tomatoes, any variety
- 1 to 1 ½ cups olive oil
- 1 head of garlic cloves, peeled
- 1 garden jalapeño, Fresno or Anaheim chili
- 1 dried Ancho chili
- salt and pepper
- 1 bunch of fresh basil

1. Chop tomatoes and spread out on 2 large sheet pans
2. Sprinkle with oil, garlic, fresh and dried chilies, and a pinch of salt.
3. Cook at 275 for 4-6 hours until a little shriveled looking and caramelized on the edges.
4. Remove from oven and let cool slightly.
5. Scoop tomato mixture into a pot and smush with a potato masher. Taste and add salt and pepper to your desired level. Serve over pasta of your choice.

Use the remaining olive oil, which is slightly spicy and tomato scented as a great add-in to sandwiches, cold pasta salad, or hot pasta dinners. You can store in the fridge for a week.

Sicilian Spaghetti Sauce

This sauce is absolutely incredible. It smells and tastes like you always hoped and imagined spaghetti sauce would be. It's almost addictive, the kind of thing you will want to make many, many jars of and hide away in your pantry. Hoard any jars in your pantry and give as gifts to anyone within commuting distance.

Makes Many Quarts

- 20-35 pounds of fresh tomatoes, rinsed and cut in half
- 1 cup + red wine
- 1/3 cup + olive oil
- 1 head of garlic, peeled
- 1 tablespoon + Salt

fresh herbs

- 4-5 stems parsley
- 1 stem leafy sage
- 1 stem rosemary
- 3-4 stems oregano
- 4-5 stems leafy basil
- 4-5 stems thyme
- 7-10 chives
- 1 bay leaf

1. Put all the ingredients in a very large pot over low heat. Mash and mush with a potato masher as the items soften over a few hours.

2. When everything is very soft and fragrant (3-6 hours), put through a food mill using the disc with the largest holes.

3. Return to the pot and continue to cook over low heat until it is the consistency you like, and season to taste.

4. Fill unsealed jars and immediately put in the refrigerator for use within a week. Store hot water sealed (canned) jars in your pantry for up to 1 year.

✎ NOTE:

Substitute any fresh herb with a ½ teaspoon of dried herbs.

Even Better, BEST Spaghetti Sauce aka Magic Spaghetti Sauce

This sauce has a lot of 'hidden' vegetables in it, even an eggplant! Which gives this sauce the most unctuous and velvety flavor I have ever had, as well as its lighter pinkish/orange color. It's also a great option for anyone who needs a little help upping their vegetable consumption.

Makes Several Quarts

- 20-35 pounds of fresh tomatoes, stem removed, rinsed and cut in half
- 1 cup + red wine
- 1/3 cup + olive oil
- 1 head of garlic, peeled
- 1 tablespoon + salt

fresh herbs

- 4-5 stems parsley
- 1 stem leafy sage
- 1 stem rosemary
- 3-4 stems oregano
- 4-5 stems leafy basil
- 4-5 stems thyme
- 7-10 chives
- a bay leaf
- 1 cup plus 2 tablespoons olive oil.
- 1 large eggplant or 2-3 medium to small eggplant, stem removed and diced into ¾ inch chunks,
- 3 pounds zucchini and yellow squash, stem removed and diced into large chunks.

1. Put the tomatoes, red wine, olive oil, garlic, salt and herbs in a very large pot over low heat.

2. Heat 1 cups olive oil to shimmering over medium to medium-high heat in a large Dutch oven or high sided skillet. Add the eggplant and cook until golden brown.

3. Add the eggplant into the large pot with the tomatoes.

4. Add the remaining 2 tablespoons. oil to the same pan you used to cook the eggplant and add zucchini or summer squash. Cook at medium high heat until the edges of the vegetables are golden brown, and they are soft.

5. Add the vegetables into the pot with the tomatoes.

6. With a potato masher, mush the tomato and vegetable mixture as it cooks and softens over a few hours.

7. When everything is very soft and fragrant (3-6 hours), put through a food mill using the disc with the largest holes.

8. Return to the pot and continue to cook over low heat until it is the consistency you like, and season to taste.

9. Fill clean jars and immediately put in the refrigerator for use within a week. Store hot water sealed (canned) jars in your pantry for up to 18 months.

Bolognese Sauce & Lasagna Bolognese

The smell, the flavor, the appearance of this sauce is just, Oh so amazing! Heady flavors, long-cooked comfort, and fresh ingredients make this dish so exceptional. While traditional lasagna Bolognese requires handmade spinach pasta, I prefer to add chopped spinach to the filling and use no-boil lasagna noodles. The results? You save hours of time, and the taste is only marginally, if at all, different.

Serves 8

Bolognese Sauce

- ¼ cup extra virgin olive oil
- 2 tablespoons butter
- 1 small yellow onion, peeled and diced
- 2 ribs celery, diced
- 3 medium carrots, peeled and diced
- 3-5 slices sopressata, about 4 ounces, finely chopped (dried Italian salami)
- 2 chicken livers, about 3 ounces, finely chopped (super easy to do this if you pop them in the freezer for about 15 minutes before chopping)
- 1 ½ pounds ground beef chuck
- ½ pound ground turkey
- salt and freshly ground black pepper
- ¾ cup dry white wine
- 1 cup milk, hot
- 2 cups chicken stock
- 1 28-ounce canned tomatoes, crushed or pureed plum tomatoes
- 1 14-ounce canned tomatoes, diced

1. Heat oil and butter in a large Dutch oven or high sided skillet over medium high heat. Add onions and sauté until soft, but not yet brown, about 4-5 minutes.

2. Add celery and carrot and cook for about 3-4 more minutes.

3. Add salami and chicken liver, and cook, stirring with a wooden spoon, until the meat is just cooked and still a little pink.

4. Crumble the ground chuck and turkey into the pot and season to taste with salt and pepper. Break up the meat, stirring frequently with the wooden spoon, until the meat is just cooked and still a little pink, about 5 more minutes. To keep the meat tender, don't fry or try to brown the meat.

5. Stir in the wine and cook until it evaporates completely, about 3-5 minutes.

6. Reduce the heat to medium and add hot milk, stirring occasionally, until the milk evaporates, and the liquid looks clear.

7. Add the broth and canned tomatoes, bring to a simmer, reduce heat to low and gently simmer for 3 hours, stirring occasionally.

8. Season to taste with salt and pepper.

Spinach Bechamel

- 3 tablespoons butter
- 4 tablespoons sifted flour
- 2 cups hot milk
- 10 ounces frozen chopped spinach, thawed and squeezed dry
- a pinch of freshly grated nutmeg
- salt and pepper to taste

1. Melt butter in a heavy medium saucepan over medium low heat. Add the flour and whisk for 2 minutes (do not allow the butter to brown).

2. Gradually add the hot milk, whisking constantly.

3. Season with salt and pepper and stir constantly until the sauce is thick and heavy and creamy, about 15 minutes.

4. Remove from heat and stir in spinach and nutmeg until combined.

Lasagna Bolognese

- 2 tablespoons extra virgin olive oil
- 1 box no-boil lasagna noodles (1 pound)
- 5 cups Bolognese sauce
- 1 cup freshly grated parmesan cheese
- 1 recipe spinach béchamel sauce (previous page)
- salt

1. Preheat the oven to 400°. Lightly oil a 9 x 12 baking pan and set aside.
2. Line the bottom of the pan with lasagna noodles.
3. Spread evenly with 1 ½ cups Bolognese sauce, then sprinkle lightly with parmesan.
4. Add another layer of pasta, spread evenly with 1 cup béchamel, then sprinkle lightly with parmesan.
5. Repeat layers until you have 3 layers of Bolognese sauce and 2 layers of béchamel, ending the Bolognese sauce and parmesan.
6. Reserve any extra Bolognese sauce for another use.
7. Bake for 30-45 minutes until lasagna is bubbling around the edges and browned on top.
8. Allow to rest for 8-10 minutes before serving.

NOTE:

To make the BEST freshly grated Parmesan cheese. Take a fresh wedge of parmesan, chop it into pieces and blend in a food processor until ground.

Broccoli Bacon Carbonara

I love to experiment in my kitchen. I made this recipe based on a craving I one night. I cooked some bacon and some pasta. I then kept adding and changing and adding until there was a meal. It turned out so good, it became a constant family fare.

Serves 4

- 1 pound acini di pepe or orzo pasta
- ½ pound bacon
- 1 pound of baby broccoli, rapini, or regular broccoli, broken or chopped into small, bite sized florets
- 1 cup milk
- 4 ounces parmesan cheese, grated (about 1 cup)
- 6 eggs
- 1 cup reserved pasta water, from when you cook the pasta
- salt and pepper to taste

1. Fill a large pot with water and 1-2 tablespoons of salt, bring to a boil. Add the broccoli and cook for about 5 minutes, until JUST tender.

2. Remove the broccoli and place in a bowl of salty ice water. Once cool, drain and set aside. Reserve the boiling water.

3. Cook the pasta according to the package instructions, in the reserved broccoli water

4. Once cooked, scoop out a cup of the pasta water and reserve for later use. Drain pasta and set aside.

5. Meanwhile, chop the bacon into bite-sized pieces and cook in a very large saucepan or pot until crispy. The pot needs to be large enough as you will use it for the whole dish.

6. Remove bacon with a slotted spoon onto a plate lined with paper towels. Reserve the pan or pot with the bacon fat in it.

7. Whisk the milk, cheese, eggs, and a ½ teaspoon pepper in a large measuring cup.

8. Add the pasta, broccoli, milk-egg mixture, and ½ cup reserved pasta water into the pot with the bacon fat in it.

9. Cook on low heat, stirring constantly, until it thickens and the sauce sort of tightens up. To thin it to your preference, you can add more pasta water.

10. Add bacon and taste for seasoning.

11. Add salt and more pepper to taste and serve.

🖉 NOTE:

If you cannot find hazelnuts, you can use toasted pine nuts, toasted almonds or roasted salted pepitas.

Pasta with Brussels Sprouts

I do love the use of orecchiette for the pasta in this dish. Orecchiette means ears in Italian, because the pasta looks like little ears. However, you can use any short pasta with nooks and crevices for catching the delicious sauce. I've also never found a better way to eat Brussels sprouts!

Serves 6

- ¾ cup hazelnuts
- 2 ½ cups chicken stock
- 1 cup reserved pasta water
- salt
- 1 pound Brussels sprouts, halved or quartered if large
- 1 pound orecchiette pasta or any small, shelled pasta like Campanella
- 4 slices of thick cut bacon, cut into 1-inch pieces
- 6 tablespoons unsalted butter (¾ of a stick of butter)
- 1 cup freshly grated parmesan cheese, about 4 ounces
- freshly ground pepper

1. Put the nuts in a dry pan and cook on the stove on medium heat until toasted and fragrant. Let the nuts cool. Then coarsely chop them.
2. In a small saucepan, simmer chicken stock until reduced by about ¾, about 15 minutes, keep warm.
3. Bring a large pot of salted water to boil. Add the Brussels sprouts, cover and cook until crisp-tender, about 5 minutes.
4. Using a slotted spoon, remove the Brussels sprouts and pat them dry.
5. Return the water to a boil. Add the orecchiette and cook until al dente, 12-15 minutes; drain and reserve 1 cup of the pasta water.
6. Meanwhile in a large, deep skillet, cook the bacon over moderately high heat until crisp, about 6 minutes. Drain the bacon on paper towels.
7. Add the butter to the skillet and cook over moderately high heat with the bacon fat until browned and nutty, about 3 minutes.
8. Add the Brussels sprouts and hazelnuts and cook until heated through, about 2 minutes.
9. Add the orecchiette along with the reduced chicken stock, and ½ cup pasta water and simmer, stirring until the sauce is slightly absorbed, about 2 minutes.
10. If it's too dry, you can add more pasta water. Stir in ½ cup of the parmesan cheese, season with salt and pepper and transfer to a large serving bowl.
11. Garnish with the bacon and the remaining ½ cup of parmesan cheese and serve.

Ribollita - Tuscan White Bean & Vegetable Stew

There is almost nothing I enjoy more on a cold winter day than a bowl of Ribollita, which is an Italian (Tuscan, actually) vegetable stew that is characterized by its use of kale. This stew also happens to be vegan. The vegetables are rich and flavorful while being soft, but not mushy. It also has creamy cannellini beans and a little bread for depth and crunch, and it is finished with a drizzle of olive oil. This stew might be the best vehicle for consuming olive oil that I have found.

Serves 10

Beans

- 1-pound dried cannellini beans
- 8 cups water
- 2 tablespoons extra virgin olive oil
- 3 cloves peeled crushed garlic
- 6-8 fresh sage leaves
- salt and pepper

Stew

- ½ cups extra virgin olive oil, divided, plus more for serving
- 1 large yellow onion, finely chopped
- 5 carrots, peeled and thickly sliced
- 2 ribs celery, trimmed and thickly sliced
- 2 Idaho potatoes, peeled and thickly sliced
- 1 large bunch of Swiss chard, trimmed and coarsely chopped
- 1 large bunch of Italian kale, also called Tuscan kale or Lacinato kale trimmed and coarsely chopped (use curly kale if you can't find Italian kale)
- ½ small Savoy cabbage, trimmed and coarsely chopped
- 1 28-ounce canned, diced tomatoes
- ½ loaf Italian or French bread or even a baguette, a bit dry or stale
- Salt and pepper to taste.

Slow cooker cooked beans

1. Put the beans, water, garlic, sage and olive oil into your slow cooker and cook on low for 8 hours or until tender.

2. Season to taste with salt and pepper. Reserve 2 cups of the cooked beans and purée the remaining beans and cooking water.

Stove top cooked beans

1. Soak beans in water for 4-10 hours, or overnight.

2. Drain and cook in 11 cups of water, Sage, garlic, and olive oil.

3. Bring to a boil and then simmer on low for 2-3 hours until tender.

4. Season to taste with salt and pepper. Reserve 2 cups of the cooked beans and purée the remaining beans and cooking water.

Assemble the Stew

5. Heat ¼ cup of olive oil in a large Dutch oven over medium low heat. Add onion and cook until soft (15-20 minutes).

6. Add carrots, celery, potato, Swiss chard, kale, and cabbage and stir. Add tomatoes, stir, and cover.

7. Cook until all the greens are wilted, 20-30 minutes.

8. Add the liquid bean purée and simmer covered for about an hour.

9. Add bread and reserved beans, stir gently, and cook on low, covered for another 25 minutes.

10. Season to taste with salt and pepper, and then refrigerate, covered, overnight.

The Next Day

1. Preheat the oven to 375 degrees. Cook soup in an oven proof casserole or Dutch oven, uncovered for 40 minutes, stirring occasionally.

2. Then cook for another 30 minutes without stirring.

3. Serve and pass with olive oil on the side.

Chapter Three

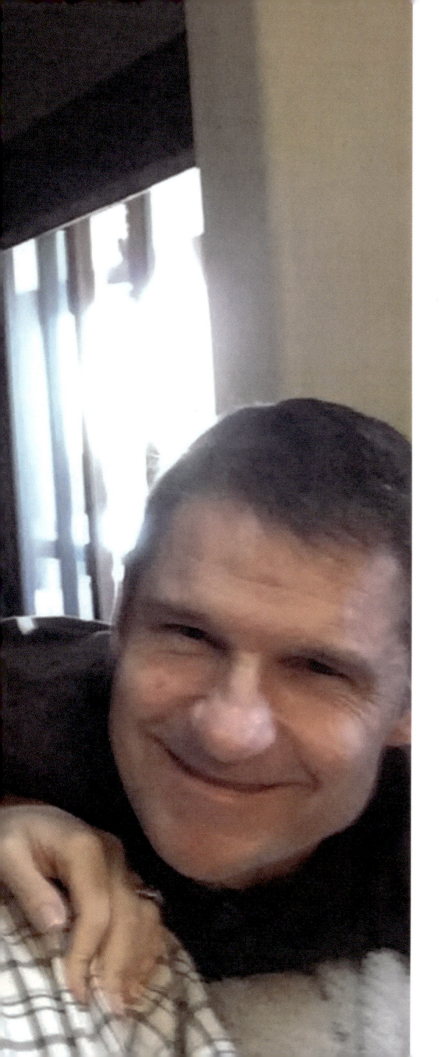

Meals You Always Want

These reliable standbys are the comfort foods that heal broken hearts, celebrate new babies, and ring in birthdays, anniversaries, promotions, and random Tuesdays with equal love and flair. Your next favorite dinner is on this list, but which one will it be? There is one way to find out…

"We can't become what we need to be by remaining what we are."

– OPRAH WINFREY

Meals You Always Want

1. Fennel Chicken 62
2. Fried Chicken 63
3. Chicken Tenderloins with White Wine butter Sauce 64
4. Vacation Chicken 66
5. Chicken & Dumplings 68
6. Fish Tacos 70
7. Skirt Steak 73
8. Enchilada Sauce & Enchiladas 74
9. Green Chicken Enchiladas 76
10. Pizza Crust & Pizza 78
11. Kale & Sausage Pie 80
12. Slow Cooker Turkey Breast 82
13. Award-winning Shrimp Pad Thai 83
14. Choucroute Garnie 84
15. Chicken Pot Pie 85
16. Cream of Tomato Soup 89
17. Butternut Squash & Roasted Fall Vegetables Soup 90
18. New Mexico Green Chili Stew 93
19. Green Smoothie 95

Fennel Chicken

This is a meal that literally makes me giddy. I love it so much.
Buttery, crispy, juicy and just so amazing and flavorful. A treat for all the senses. All of this and it has NO butter or oil of any kind. Also, the skin on the chicken is part of the gorgeous delight, it comes out crispy and thick with salt and seasonings, making it almost like croutons!

Serves 5

- 1 whole chicken
- 2 tablespoons kosher salt
- 1 tablespoon fennel seeds
- 2 tablespoons herbes de Provence

1. Preheat the oven to 425 degrees.
2. Blend the spices in a spice grinder or food processor until ground up, but not fine like a powder.
3. Cover the chicken inside and out with the spice mixture. And let sit at room temperature for an hour.
4. Cook the chicken in a 5 or 7 quart Dutch oven (enameled cast iron is the best option as it retains the heat the best when cooking) for 1 hour and 10 minutes.
5. Turn off the oven, crack the door and let it sit for 20 minutes.
6. Let rest on your cutting board, covered for another 10 minutes. Carve and serve.

✎ NOTE:

You can use the coating on chicken parts. Coat and let rest for 20 minutes instead of a full hour. Cook on a rack placed over a cookie sheet for about 40 minutes or until juices run clear, when pierced with a knife.

Fried Chicken

It starts with an appealing sizzle. That crackly sound when you place the floured raw chicken parts into the hot oil. And there is that occasional big POP when a drop of water eeks out into the oil. Combine that sound with the heady smell of yummy, juicy, crispy fried chicken and I'm carried all the way back to my childhood. When I was a young girl, my parents would make and serve fried chicken and buttermilk biscuits for dinner every Sunday night. This is that chicken with a heady smell, primal taste, crackly sounds and finger licking yummy goodness!

Serves 4

- 4 pounds skin-on, bone-in chicken parts – I use legs and thighs
- 4 quarts water
- ¾ cup kosher salt
- 3 cups flour
- 1 tablespoon sweet paprika
- 1 teaspoon smoked paprika
- 1 tablespoon salt
- 2 teaspoon pepper
- canola oil for frying
- 2-3 tablespoons bacon fat

NOTE:

Store leftovers in a brown paper bag. This helps to preserve some of the crispness. Reheat in the oven, air fryer, or in a dry pan on the stove with the lid, but not the microwave if you want to retain the crispy coating.

1. Brine the chicken pieces in 4 quarts of water with ¾ cups of kosher salt, covered, for an hour. Make sure the brine stays cold by keeping it in the refrigerator or adding ice to it.
2. In a zip top bag, put 3 cups of flour, sweet paprika, smoked paprika, salt and pepper and shake.
3. Use tongs to remove the chicken from the brine and shake in the flour mixture, about 3-4 pieces at a time, and then place on a wire rack that is placed over a cookie sheet to catch the flour that falls off.
4. When all the chicken pieces have been floured, let sit for 15 minutes and then re-flour all of them by shaking them in the bag again. This makes the chicken extra crispy.
5. Throw the seasoned flour and shaking bag away.
6. Put ½ inch canola oil in an electric skillet and let heat to 375 degrees. Add 2-3 Tablespoons of bacon fat for flavor. I save bacon fat in an old clean mustard jar and store it in the refrigerator.
7. Fry chicken pieces, partially covered, 13-15 minutes per side or until golden. Don't crowd the pan.
8. Remove to a large platter lined with paper towels. Enjoy!

Chicken Tenderloins with White Wine Butter Sauce

If you have ever had classic French escargots with sizzled garlic parsley butter, then you know, they are amazing, but it's the butter that makes the dish, it's the best part! This recipe is for those of you who desperately love that flavor and want to experience it without the snails. This is a delightfully flavored, juicy and decadent meal. I love it with a fresh and crusty French baguette and some angel hair pasta. What a great way to have more sauce!

Serves 4

- 4 boneless skinless Chicken breasts
- 2 teaspoons Olive oil
- ¼ cup dry white wine
- ½ cup chicken broth
- 1 tablespoon white wine vinegar or more to taste
- salt and pepper

Garlic parsley butter

- ½ cup (1 stick) butter softened to room temperature
- 3 tablespoons parsley, chopped fine
- 2 cloves garlic, chopped fine
- 1 teaspoon cognac
- 1 tablespoon dry white wine

✎ NOTE:

Make a double batch of butter and keep it in the freezer for use when needed.

1. Make the butter. Use a fork to mash and blend butter, parsley, garlic, cognac and wine.

2. Once it's all incorporated, put it in the refrigerator to cure. The flavors will develop in about an hour.

3. For this recipe, you can use it straight from the refrigerator. You can also make up to a month ahead of time and freeze the butter. When you are ready to use it, simply remove it from the freezer about an hour or 2 before you need it. This recipe uses half the butter, and you can reserve the other half in the freezer for the next time.

4. Salt and pepper your chicken breasts. Sauté the chicken in Dutch oven or large skillet that can accommodate all the chicken at once on medium heat in 2 teaspoons olive oil until golden brown on each side.

5. Remove the chicken from the pan and put on a plate. Cover with foil to keep warm.

6. Turn the skillet back onto medium, add the broth and wine, and simmer until reduced by half while scraping up any brown bits in the pan with a wooden spoon.

7. Add the chicken back in, put a lid on, and cook at medium low until the breasts are cooked through and nice and juicy. This should take about 10-20 minutes depending on the size of the pieces of chicken.

8. Once it's cooked, remove the chicken back to the plate and cover.

9. Then make the sauce-Reduce the skillet to low heat, and whisk in the butter, 1 tablespoon at a time until completely emulsified before adding the next tablespoon.

10. Once all the butter has been blended in, whisk in the vinegar.

11. Taste the sauce. Add salt and pepper if needed.

12. Serve the chicken with the sauce poured on top.

Vacation Chicken

I have a close-knit group of friends with whom I have gone on multiple girls' trips. On our very first trip, we were maneuvering through dinner planning when my friend Susan volunteered to make baked chicken one of the nights. We all loved the idea, especially because we all know Susan to be a great cook. This chicken was named Vacation Chicken that first night she made it, and it remains our favorite meal of every trip we take.

Serves 6

- 3-4 Pounds of chicken legs and thighs, skin-on, bone-in
- salt and pepper to taste
- ¼ cup Dijon mustard
- 1 cup panko breadcrumbs
- 3 tablespoons melted butter
- ¾ cup white wine
- ½ cup chicken stock

1. Preheat the oven to 375°. Dry and then salt and pepper all the chicken pieces. Place them in a 9 x 13 glass baking dish and spread the mustard on the tops of the pieces.
2. Toss the breadcrumbs in the melted butter, and then coat the top of the chicken pieces in the buttery breadcrumbs.
3. Drizzle the white wine and broth in the pan to avoid getting the breadcrumbs wet.
4. Cover with foil and bake for 45-55 minutes.
5. Remove foil and cook for another 15 minutes or until the breadcrumbs are golden and crispy and the chicken juices run clear when pierced with a knife. If they need extra crisping, you can put them under the broiler for a minute or 2.

NOTE:

Use gluten free breadcrumbs for a completely gluten free dish.

Chicken & Dumplings

There's nothing better on a cold rainy day than chicken and dumplings! Warm and satisfying, burgeoning with vegetables, teamed with moist, juicy chicken and fluffy dumplings.

Serves 10

- 1 whole fully cooked rotisserie chicken, deboned and shredded into larger bite-sized pieces. Save the carcass to make your own chicken stock.
- 1 onion
- 3 stalks celery, chopped into ¾ inch pieces
- 4 medium carrots, chopped into ¾ inch pieces
- 4 tablespoons butter
- 6 tablespoons flour
- 2 quarts chicken stock
- 1 cup heavy cream
- 3 sprigs of fresh thyme leaves, stripped off the stems, about a tablespoon
- salt and pepper
- 2 tablespoons sherry
- ¾ cup frozen peas
- ½ cup flat leaf parsley, chopped

Dumplings

- 2 cups flour
- 1 teaspoon kosher salt
- 1 tablespoon baking soda
- 1 cup milk
- 3 tablespoons butter

1. Bring ½ inch water to simmer in a pot fitted with a steamer basket. Add celery, carrots, and chopped onions.

2. Cover and steam until just tender, about 10-12 minutes. Remove and set aside.

3. For the dumplings, mix the flour, baking powder, and salt in a medium bowl.

4. Heat butter and milk until steaming in a glass measuring cup in the microwave and add to dry ingredients.

5. Mix with a fork until the dough barely comes together, about 3-4 times around the bowl and set aside.

6. Heat the butter in a 7-quart, or larger Dutch oven or pot over medium high heat.

7. Whisk in the flour and thyme and continue whisking and cooking until the flour turns a golden color, which takes a couple of minutes.

8. While whisking, add the sherry and then the chicken stock.

9. Simmer until the gravy thickens a little (about 3-4 minutes). Stir in the cream, chicken and steamed vegetables and return to a simmer.

10. Scoop the dumplings onto the surface of the simmering soup using a tablespoon sized scoop. They will double in size while they cook.

11. If the scoop gets sticky, dip in the hot soup and keep scooping until all the dumplings are in the pot.

12. Cover and simmer on low or medium low heat for 15-20 minutes until the dumplings are cooked through.

13. Gently stir in the peas and parsley.

14. Add generous amounts of salt and pepper to taste. Serve.

✎ NOTE:

Omit the dumplings and serve over rice or noodles.

Fish Tacos

I was transformed the first time I had fish tacos in Los Angeles with my brother. They were so flavorful and so very satisfying! I was full, satiated, but not uncomfortably full. It was my kind of meal! So, I just had to learn an easy way to make them at home, and here it is!

Serves 6

Fish

- 4 filets of tilapia, sole, flounder, cod or other mild white flaky fish
- 1 ½ cups flour
- ½ cup cornstarch
- 2 teaspoons kosher Salt
- ½ teaspoon pepper
- About 1 cup of oil, for cooking. Anything that tolerates high heat is great, like peanut oil, grapeseed oil, canola oil, or even vegetable oil.
- 1 lime, cut into 6-8 wedges

Sriracha slaw

- ½ head green cabbage, cleaned, cored and sliced thin
- 1 teaspoon Sriracha (or more if you want it spicier)
- ¾ cup mayonnaise
- ½ teaspoon salt

Quick pickled onions

- 1 red or yellow onion, peeled and sliced thin
- juice of one lime
- 1 teaspoon salt
- ¼ teaspoon pepper

Beans

- 1 can black beans
- 1 teaspoon cumin
- 1 teaspoon minced garlic
- ½ teaspoon salt
- Small flour tortillas, about 12, warmed

1. For the slaw, mix the mayonnaise, Sriracha, salt and pepper in a bowl large enough to accommodate the sauce and the cabbage. Toss the sauce with the thin sliced cabbage and set aside until everything else is ready.

2. For the pickled onions, toss the onions, lime juice, salt and pepper in a medium bowl and set aside until everything else is ready. They will pickle in about 10 minutes.

3. For the beans, put a saucepan on the stove on low and add the drained beans, cumin, garlic, salt, and pepper. Heat, stirring occasionally, until warmed through and set aside until everything else is ready.

4. For the fish, chop the filets into large chunks, about an inch to an inch and half wide.

5. Put the flour, cornstarch, salt and pepper into a bag that's large enough to accommodate all the fish. Toss the fish in the bag to coat.

6. Put about half an inch of oil in a large skillet on medium heat. Cook the fish once the oil is hot until lightly golden on each side. It should take just a couple of minutes per side, depending on the thickness of your fish.

7. Once the fish is cooked remove it from the oil onto a paper towel lined plate and lightly salt. Set it aside until everything else is ready.

8. To assemble, fill warmed tortillas with the slaw, beans, pickled onions, and fish.

9. Serve with a lime wedge on the side!

✎ Note:

Fish Taco Rice bowls are a wonderful dinner or lunch option. Omit the tortillas and make jasmine rice instead. Layer rice and all other toppings in bowls. Serve with chopsticks.

Skirt Steak

Skirt steak is one of my favorite stand-by, for cocktail parties and get togethers. These small portions of deliciously marinated flavorful meat are a very nice complement to a veggie tray, chips and dip, some cheese and crackers and maybe some hummus.

Serves 4

- 1 ½ – 3 pounds skirt steak, depending on how much you want to make
- 3 tablespoons soy sauce
- 1 tablespoon brown sugar
- 1 teaspoon salt
- ½ teaspoon black pepper
- ½ teaspoon dried oregano
- ½ teaspoon garlic powder or 1 garlic clove crushed
- ¼ cups canola oil, vegetable oil or grapeseed oil

1. Combine all dry ingredients in a jar and shake. I use an old clean glass mustard jar.
2. Pour the marinade over the meat in a zipper bag and refrigerate for at least 30 minutes, or up to a day and a half.
3. Grill on medium hot grill for 2-4 minutes per side, depending on the thickness of the meat and your grill.
4. Let the meat rest, covered, on a plate for about 10 minutes before cutting to allow the juices to redistribute. Serve and enjoy!

Enchilada Sauce

October is the month of harvest! I'm not just talking about our loaded and waning vegetable gardens, I'm also talking about things like wine grapes, truffles and an item close to my heart and roots: Hatch Chili Peppers from my dad's hometown, Hatch, New Mexico. Hatch red chili powder is no joke in my family, nor is the family enchilada sauce recipe made from it. This recipe, handed down from dad's Aunt Opal, and our enchilada-making approach has been in our family for generations. We love our rich red spicy, smooth, deep and pure flavorful enchilada sauce, and I hope you do too!

Yield-5 pints

- 1 cup flour
- 1 cup bacon fat, or lard or shortening
- 1 cup Hatch, NM red chili powder, choose the heat when you purchase!
- 8 cups chicken stock
- salt and pepper to taste

1. In a large Dutch oven at medium heat, melt the bacon fat and add the flour, whisking often, until the roux has thinned out a little and turned a warm brown color.

2. Whisk in the chili powder until smooth. Do NOT bend over the pot and breathe in the aroma, it will burn.

3. Whisk in 8 cups of chicken stock and simmer on low, stirring often, until it thickens. Taste it for seasoning and adjust as needed.

4. Store in the refrigerator for about a week, in the freezer for 6 months or canned for a year. If canning it, do it in a pressure canner (approx. 45 minutes) at 10 pounds for half pints if you live at sea level. If you live at a higher altitude, please consult your own resources for canning meat stock.

Enchiladas

Serves 4

- 8 corn tortillas
- 1 pound ground beef
- 1 clove garlic, put through a garlic press
- salt
- 2 cups of shredded cheddar or Mexican blend cheese
- 1 small yellow onion, chopped
- 1 cup of enchilada sauce (1 half-pint jar)
- 4 eggs at room temperature
- 2- 4 tablespoons canola, vegetable or grapeseed oil

1. Preheat the oven to 250 degrees.
2. In a saucepan, cook the ground beef with the garlic and salt to taste, breaking it up often with a spoon or spatula, until no longer pink.
3. Remove from heat and set aside.
4. In a small skillet, warm 2 tsp oil until hot. Heat each corn tortilla for about 30 seconds on each side. Let them sit on the side on paper towels until ready to assemble the enchiladas.
5. Place a tortilla on an oven proof plate
6. Top with about ¼ cups of beef, a sprinkling of raw onion, cheese and enchilada sauce.
7. Top with another tortilla and repeat the toppings.
8. Put the plate in the oven so the cheese can melt.
9. Build 3 more plates.
10. When all plates are in the oven, fry the eggs sunny side up, top with salt and pepper.
11. Remove the plates from the oven and place an egg on top of each enchilada. Serve immediately.

✎ NOTE:

These are instructions for a standard 'double enchilada'. Modify your taste by building a triple or quad layer and double the sauce.

Green Chicken Enchiladas

I always wanted to create a homemade, spicy and healthy green chicken enchilada. Once I made this recipe, it very quickly became a sought-after staple at my farmstand. It's the wonderfully flavored and spicy sauce that makes it great!

Serves 6

Sauce

- 10 large fresh poblano peppers
- 1 medium white onion, peeled and chopped
- 1 teaspoon chopped garlic
- 1 tablespoon vegetable or avocado oil
- 1/3 cup flour, or your favorite gluten-free flour blend
- 4 cups chicken broth
- 3 fresh jalapenos, stemmed and chopped coarsely, leave the seeds in them unless you want to remove some of the spiciness in the sauce. Less seeds means less spicy.
- 2 four-ounce cans green chilies
- 1 teaspoon kosher salt
- 1 teaspoon black pepper
- 1 teaspoon cayenne pepper
- 1 teaspoon ground cumin
- 1 teaspoon oregano

1. Turn the oven on to broil and line a large cookie sheet with foil.
2. Place the poblano peppers on the sheet and cook 5-10 minutes on each side, until the skins blacken. If there are still some green sections showing, that's good. You don't want to burn and dry them out. The flesh of the peppers should be green and slightly tender.
3. Let them cool. Once they are cool, remove the stems and most of the seeds. It's fine if some seeds remain.
4. While the peppers are cooling, put the oil in a large Dutch oven at medium low heat.
5. Add the chopped onion and garlic and cook until the onion is softened.
6. Add the flour and stir until no white remains and slightly cooked, about 2 minutes.
7. Whisk in the chicken broth, and then add the green chilies, jalapenos, and poblano peppers and stir.
8. Add the salt, pepper, cayenne, oregano and cumin and bring to a simmer, stirring occasionally.
9. Cook until the jalapenos have softened, about 20-30 minutes. Remove from the heat.
10. Pour it into a blender to puree. Add salt and pepper seasoning to taste.

Assemble the Enchiladas

- 4 cups green enchilada sauce (see recipe above)
- 1 package 6–9-inch Corn tortillas
- 1 cup Monterey Jack cheese
- 1 pound cooked, chopped rotisserie chicken

Into a 9x13 inch glass baking dish, layer the ingredients as follows. Start with 1 cup enchilada sauce, then top with a layer of tortillas, then sauce, then cheese, then chicken. Repeat the tortilla, sauce, cheese chicken 2 more times. The top with tortillas, sauce and cheese.

Bake at 350 for 45 minutes or until bubbly and golden brown in spots.

Pizza Crust & Pizza

I love pizza. I spent a few years in Tuscany, Italy and came back loving pizza even more than I did when I left. Learning to make the elusive thin crusted, not too crispy, not too soft pizza crust was a goal I had after returning. This pizza dough can be made in several batches, wrapped in plastic and stored in the freezer. Simply move a ball to the fridge and you can throw together a fresh homemade pizza dinner in minutes.

Makes 3 Pizzas

- 1/2 cup warm water (around 110 degrees, which is lukewarm to the touch)
- 1 tablespoon yeast
- 1 ¼ cups room temperature water (65-80 degrees)
- 2 tablespoons extra virgin olive oil
- 4 cups high gluten flour (or bread flour), plus more for dusting the surface
- 1 ½ teaspoons salt

1. Measure the ½ cups warm water into a two-cups liquid measure cup.
2. Sprinkle in the yeast and let stand until it dissolves and swells, about 5 minutes. Add the room temperature water and oil and stir to combine.
3. Process the flour and salt in a large food processor, pulsing to combine.
4. Continue pulsing while pouring the liquid ingredients (holding back a few tablespoons). If the dough does not readily form into a ball, add the remaining liquid and continue to pulse until the ball forms.
5. Process until the dough is smooth and elastic, about 30 seconds longer.
6. The dough will be a bit tacky, so use a rubber spatula to turn it out onto a lightly floured work surface.
7. Knead by hand for a few strokes to form a smooth, round ball.
8. Put the dough ball into a deep oiled bowl and cover with plastic wrap.
9. If you are freezing for a later use, wrap the ball in plastic instead and place it in your freezer.
10. Let rise until doubled in size, 1 ½ -2 hours.
11. Press the dough to deflate it.
12. When you are ready to make your pizza, turn the oven on to 500 degrees for at least 30 minutes.
13. Cut each ball into three pieces and toss it around a little bit of flour and then cover it with a damp cloth and let it relax for about 20 minutes.

14. Roll or stretch each piece of dough into a 9-to-11 inch circle and place on parchment paper scattered with cornmeal or flour.

15. Top with sauce and / or toppings of your choice.

16. Slide the Pizza onto a heated pizza stone using your pizza peel if you have one.

17. Alternately, bake on a baking sheet lined with parchment paper and scattered with a little flour or cornmeal.

18. Bake until the crust begins to brown in spots, 6 -10 minutes. If you choose not to put toppings on you might need to prick the dough with a fork before it goes in the oven so that it doesn't get a big bubble While it's cooking.

19. Let it rest for 5-10 minutes after it comes out of the oven before you dig in!

✎ NOTE:

This dough is very versatile. You can roll it out and fill it like your favorite calzone, go sweet or savory. Try things like cinnamon sugar, fruit and sugar, potatoes and onions, oil and herbs, cheese and meat, vegetables and cheese, and so much more.

Kale & Sausage Pie

Kale is deep green and rich in iron and other vitamins. I have a bunch of it growing in little tucked away parts of the garden at my house. It grows year-round in many places, and not only can it survive frost, but the cold also actually sweetens the flavor somewhat. One great way to use kale is in a kale pie, which is really like quiche. It's loaded with eggs, cheeses, sausage, kale, sweet potato and shallots, all encased in a buttery flaky pie crust. This pie is so hearty and delicious.

Serves 10

- 1 recipe for double crust pie crust
- 2 pounds kale, or a mix of kale, Swiss chard, beet greens, and / or escarole. At least half of the mix should be kale. Clean, blanch (cook for 4 minutes in salted boiling water), drain, dry, then chop.
- 1 tablespoon olive oil
- 2 tablespoons butter
- 1 shallot, minced
- 1 clove minced garlic
- 1 ½ cups shredded cheese: mozzarella or a mix of mozzarella and parmesan or pecorino
- 1 cup cubed fresh mozzarella
- 1 cup ricotta cheese, drained
- 1-pound sausages, fully cooked and sliced
- 4 whole eggs plus 1 egg yolk
- ½ pound sweet potatoes, peeled and chopped
- ½ cup heavy cream
- salt and pepper to taste
- an additional egg, to top the pie.

Double Pie Crust

- 3 cups flour
- 1 tablespoon sugar
- 1 teaspoon salt
- ½ cup butter, cold and cut into pieces (1/4 pound)
- 1 cup shortening
- 10-16 tablespoons ice water

1. Combine flour, sugar, salt, butter and shortening in a bowl using 2 butter knives or a pastry blender until the butter and shortening are the size of small peas.

2. Add 10 tablespoons of ice water and mix in with a fork to form a ball. If it's too dry to form a ball, dribble in more ice water, 1 tablespoon at a time until it comes together.

3. Knead the ball 4-5 times, return to the bowl, cover and refrigerate for at least 30 minutes. The colder the dough is, the easier it is to work with.

4. Shape dough into a ball, cover with plastic wrap, and put in the refrigerator for at least 30 minutes (colder is better here). This can be done up to 2 days before use.

5. When ready, remove from the fridge, divide in 2, and roll each into a circle large enough to fit your pan with about an inch or inch and half hanging over the side. I use a very large pie pan (I use a 11 inch pan with straight sides, so it can hold a lot).

6. Grease the pan and put the bottom crust in, very gently, don't stretch the dough.

Make the filling

1. Melt the oil and butter at medium heat in a sauté pan large enough to hold the greens, they will cook down. Cook the shallot and garlic until soft. Add the greens and cook until they are soft, and the liquid mostly evaporates.
2. Separately, Chop the sausage and sweet potatoes and spread out on a cookie sheet.
3. Drizzle with a tablespoon of olive oil and shake the pan to coat the items.
4. Season with a teaspoon of salt. Bake at 350 for 20 minutes or until the sweet potatoes have softened somewhat.
5. Meanwhile, combine the eggs, cheese, cream, salt and pepper in a large bowl.
6. Add in sausage mixture, greens mixture, and mix gently until combined.

Build the pie

1. Preheat the oven to 350 degrees.
2. Place the filling into the bottom crust of the pie. Lay the top crust over everything and cut four 3-inch vents in it. Whisk 1 egg and a teaspoon of water together, brush the top crust.
3. Place on a cookie sheet and bake at 350 degrees for one hour.
4. Remove from oven, slice and serve!

Slow Cooker Turkey Breast

Thanksgiving and the holiday season mean the neighborhood markets will be filling up with big boneless turkey breasts. The ones my store has in their freezer are about 4.5 pounds. So, of course I stock up! These big boneless turkey breasts are perfectly suited for cooking in the slow cooker with a few special details to make them extra delicious. The result is the best turkey cold cuts I've ever had in a sandwich. Or a delightful turkey dinner any time of year. Warm turkey atop a crisp green salad with a tangy mustard vinaigrette dressing. A turkey wrap with hummus and quinoa salad. The meat is juicy and flavorful and awesome.

Serves 4

- 1 boneless turkey breast, 3.5 – 5 pounds
- 1 onion, chopped
- 1 cup apricot jam or jelly.
- 2 tablespoons Dijon mustard
- 1 cup chicken broth
- salt and pepper to taste
- optional- chop up one apple, plum, peach, pear, stalk of celery, or nectarine and add it to the pot

1. Put everything in the pot of the slow cooker and cook for 4 to 5 hours on low.

2. Remove turkey, cool, and slice according to your preference. If you like the meat sliced thin, it's easier to do once it has been refrigerated.

3. The sauce in the slow cooker is delicious with the meat and makes it extra moist and flavorful.

Award-winning Shrimp Pad Thai

I was a teenager when I had my first taste of Pad Thai, and it was life changing! I loved the explosion of flavors and texture. After many versions and tweaks I eventually crafted my own Pad Thai with Shrimp using mostly mainstream ingredients, and of course the fish sauce. This very sauce was given an award by the awareness campaign for Asian Pacific American Forum, which is a network that supports and provides networking opportunities for Asian pacific Americans at work. It went on to be served in my work cafeteria with the other recipe winners!

Serves 4

- 4 tablespoons peanut oil
- 1 tablespoon crushed garlic
- 1 pound raw shrimp / prawns, cleaned
- 2 eggs, lightly beaten
- ½ pound flat rice noodles, cooked as directed until al dente
- 1 cup purple cabbage, chopped
- ¼ cup chopped cilantro or arugula
- ¼ cup peanuts, chopped
- 4 scallions, thinly sliced
- 2 limes, cut into wedges
- 3 tablespoons water
- ¼ cup fish sauce
- 3 tablespoons ketchup
- 2 tablespoons sugar
- ½ chopped tomato

1. Make the sauce by mixing the water, fish sauce, ketchup, sugar, and tomatoes in a bowl and set aside.
2. Heat a saucepan over high heat.
3. Add 2 tablespoons peanut oil, garlic and shrimp and cook until the shrimp are opaque.
4. Remove the shrimp from the pan with tongs or a slotted spoon and reserve on a plate.
5. In the same pan, add 2 remaining tablespoons peanut oil, reduce the heat to medium, and scramble eggs until cooked but still tender.
6. Add sauce and noodles to the pan and toss until well-mixed.
7. Add purple cabbage and shrimp and mix again.
8. Place on a serving platter or individual plates and garnish with cilantro, peanuts, scallions and lime wedges.

✎ NOTE:

You can easily replace the shrimp with chicken tenders, 1 pound, cut into 1-inch pieces. Additionally, Purple cabbage turns everything blue when you save these as a leftover for the next day, don't worry, it's still amazing!

Choucroute Garnie

Choucroute Garnie is a slow braised pork and sauerkraut dish with apples and onions and white wine. The tanginess of the fermented cabbage provides an amazing acidic balance with the long cooking process blending the apples, onions and spices to create a flavorful and rich dish. This is an old recipe from the Alsace region of France, which explains the use of pork and sausages and sauerkraut, as it is geographically quite close to Germany, as well as the use of fruity dry white wine, which is typical to Alsace-Lorraine, France. *For Sue.*

Serves 12

- 2 tablespoons olive oil
- 2 medium yellow onions, chopped
- 4 medium green apples, preferably Granny Smith, cored, quartered and sliced
- salt and pepper
- 1 bay leaf
- 2 tablespoons chopped fresh parsley
- 1 teaspoon dried coriander
- 1 teaspoon dried thyme
- 1 tablespoon garlic, chopped
- 3 cups fruity but dry white wine
- 4 pounds pork - smoked ham hocks, bratwurst, or other cooked sausages, pork shoulder or ham bone
- 3 pounds sauerkraut, fresh, not canned

1. Preheat the oven to 350 degrees Fahrenheit. Put a large Dutch oven over medium heat and add the olive oil.
2. Sauté onions and apples until soft and then add salt and pepper, garlic, bay leaf, parsley, coriander, and thyme.
3. Let the spices warm for about one minute and then add the wine, pork, and sauerkraut.
4. Bring it up to a simmer and then put the lid on and put it in the oven for 2 hours.
5. Serve hot. It pairs very well with roasted or mashed potatoes.

NOTE:

If pork isn't your thing, you can make this with chicken. Use dark meat only (raw chicken thighs and chicken sausages are ideal) and reduce the cooking time in the oven to one hour.

Chicken Pot Pie

When I started making dinners for the farmstand, this chicken pot pie was the front runner. It's a popular grab and go dinner for my customers. Deciding to figure out how to make chicken pot pie, made me grow to truly love it. This recipe doesn't even require being put into a pastry crust, eat it as a soup and vary the vegetables by the season!

Makes 1 Pie, with leftover filling to use as soup

- 1 recipe for double crust pie crust
- 2 teaspoons vegetable oil
- ½ teaspoon dried thyme
- 1 teaspoon kosher salt
- ½ teaspoon fresh cracked black pepper
- ½ pound carrots
- 1 stalk celery
- 1-pound potatoes
- 1 medium onion
- 1 cup green beans, chopped into 1-inch lengths
- 1 medium stick of zucchini
- 1 medium stick of yellow squash
- 1 cup frozen peas
- 2 pounds chicken
- ½ cup parsley
- 5 cups chicken broth
- 2 tablespoons heavy cream
- 2 tablespoons sherry

Double Pie Crust

- 3 cups flour
- 1 tablespoon sugar
- 1 teaspoon salt
- ½ cup butter, cold and cut into pieces (½ stick)
- 1 cup shortening
- 10-16 tablespoons ice water

1. Combine flour, sugar, salt, butter and shortening in a bowl using 2 butter knives or a pastry blender until the butter and shortening are the size of small peas.

2. Add 10 tablespoons of ice water and mix in with a fork to form a ball. If it's too dry to form a ball, dribble in more ice water, 1 tablespoon at a time until it comes together.

3. Knead the ball 4-5 times, return to the bowl, cover and refrigerate for at least 30 minutes. The colder the dough is, the easier it is to work with.

4. Shape dough into a ball, cover with plastic wrap, and put in the refrigerator for at least 30 minutes (colder is better here). This can be done up to 2 days before use.

Make the filling

1. Put the vegetable oil in a large pot that can hold your entire batch easily, at least 4 quarts. Turn the heat to medium and add the carrots, potatoes, onions, green beans, celery, salt, pepper, and thyme.

2. When those ingredients start to soften, add the chopped zucchini and yellow squash and cook for about 5 more minutes.

3. Then add the flower and stir with a wooden spoon until no white remains, about 2 minutes.

4. Add the Sherry and stir it in for about a minute.

5. Add the chicken broth and simmer gently until the vegetables are pleasantly tender but not too soft.

6. Add the chicken, parsley, and frozen peas, and cook 5-15 more minutes until everything is incorporated.

7. Turn off the heat and add the cream. Taste. Adjust salt and pepper to your taste.

8. Package and refrigerate or freeze it until you are ready to use it as soup or pie filling.

Build the pie

1. Preheat the oven to 375 degrees.

2. Cut your pie dough into a 2/3 portion and a 1/3 portion. The larger part for the bottom, and the smaller part for the top.

3. Dust your countertop or your parchment if you want to keep your countertop clean with flower roll out the bottom pie dough a couple of inches larger than the size of your pie pan.

4. Spray your pie pan with cooking spray, lay the pie dough into the pan and pinch the edge all the way around the edge.

5. Fill the bottom of the pie dough with your chicken pot pie filling. I like to let it pile up just a little bit.

6. Roll out the top pie dough a little larger than the pan. Place it on top of your pie and then pinch it with your fingers so that it has little mountains and crevices in it.

7. Sprinkle the top pie crust with a pinch of salt and pepper.

8. Put your pie pan on a cookie sheet to catch any drips and cook it in the oven at 375 degrees for 45 minutes until it is golden and bubbling.

✎ NOTE:

Some fun add-ins to this recipe are sauteed mushrooms, summer corn, slivered toasted almonds and cooked broccoli.

 **NOTE:**

Don't have a slow cooker? Use your oven, set at 200 degrees, cover and cook for about 4 hours.

Cream of Tomato Soup

I find tomato soup, when it's done well, to be remarkably comforting. I even warm it up in a coffee mug as my breakfast sometimes. This is, without a doubt, the most delicious tomato soup. It's incredibly light on the cream but it still has that deep creamy taste and texture.

Yield – 7 quarts

- 1 medium onion, chopped
- I stick salted butter (8 tablespoons)
- ½ cup brown sugar
- 1-6 ounce can tomato paste
- 1 teaspoon salt
- ½ teaspoon pepper
- 1 cup flour
- 12 cups canned, diced tomatoes and their juice (#10 can)
- 12 cups of the diced tomatoes liquid, adding vegetable or chicken stock to make 12 cups
- 3 Bay Leaves
- ½ cup cream
- 3 tablespoons sherry
- pinch cayenne pepper

1. In a large enough pot to hold the ingredients or in your slow cooker insert if it is stovetop compatible, melt the butter over medium high heat.
2. Once melted, add the chopped onion, brown sugar, tomato paste, salt, and pepper.
3. Once the onion has softened, add the strained diced tomatoes from the can, making sure to reserve their juice. Cook these items over the cooktop, stirring frequently, until most of the liquid is gone and the tomatoes and onions start to caramelize a little bit.
4. Add the flour, stir until no white pockets remain.
5. Add the broth and juice and stir until smooth and no longer clumpy.
6. Then add the Bay leaves and put into your slow cooker, covered, on low for seven hours.
7. Once it has been cooked, remove the bay leaves and discard them.
8. Then, puree the ingredients. You can use an immersion blender, or you can do it in batches in your food processor or blender. Careful not to overfill the blender as the ingredients are very hot.
9. Then put the pureed soup back into your pot and add the cream with Sherry and the cayenne pepper. Don't omit the cayenne pepper; it adds a lot of flavor and not a lot of spice.
10. Taste and add additional salt and pepper as desired.
11. Serve and enjoy!
12. Once cooled it can be frozen and enjoyed on a future date.

Butternut Squash & Roasted Fall Vegetables Soup

I love that winter squash has a hard shell and can store all winter in a cool place, like your root cellar, or garage or basement or something. I love that it sweetens as you store it, and I love this soup. The addition of the beets makes it a gorgeous color and adds a well-rounded earthy depth of flavor that is so delicious.

Serves 6

- 3 tablespoons unsalted butter
- 6 sage leaves
- 1 cup finely chopped onion (about 2 onions)
- 1 recipe roasted fall vegetables
- 2 cups chicken broth
- 1 cup water
- salt and freshly ground pepper to taste
- 1 cup milk
- ½ cup heavy cream
- ¼ teaspoon freshly grated nutmeg
- 1/8 teaspoon cayenne or to taste

1. Heat the butter in a medium size pot and add the crushed sage leaves and onion.
2. Cook over medium heat, stirring, for 1 minute.
3. Add the roasted fall vegetables, chicken broth, water, salt and pepper.
4. Bring the mixture to a boil, reduce to a simmer, and cook for about 20 minutes.
5. Transfer to the bowl of an electric blender or food processor and puree until smooth. Return the mixture to the pot.
6. Add the milk and half-and-half, nutmeg, cayenne, salt and freshly ground black pepper. Stir well and simmer for 5 to 10 minutes.
7. Taste for seasoning and serve!

Roasted Fall Vegetables

- 1 medium butternut squash
- 1 acorn squash
- 1 medium to large beet
- 1 large yellow onion
- 3 large carrots
- 10-12 fresh sage leaves
- 6 cloves garlic, peeled
- 4 sprigs fresh thyme
- 3 tbsp olive oil
- salt and pepper

1. Preheat the oven to 400°. Line a cookie sheet with foil and coat lightly with cooking spray.

2. Peel squashes and remove seeds. Cut into large chunks, about 4-6 pieces each and place on the cookie sheet.

3. Peel the onion and cut into quarters.

4. Wash carrots and trim off the ends.

5. Add the onion and carrots along with the garlic, herbs, oil, salt and pepper to the cookie sheet and toss to coat.

6. Trim and rinse the beet, place in a foil packet, unpeeled, drizzled with olive oil and salt. Place on the pan with everything else.

7. Roast everything for an hour.

8. Remove vegetables from the oven. Discard the thyme stems. Save everything else. The sage and thyme leaves will be crispy and the garlic should be soft and sweet.

9. Let the beet cool until you can touch it. Peel it and discard the peels.

Note:

Soup "Sips" are a very fun feature at cocktail parties. Keep your soup warm and serve it with a small ladle and espresso cups. Serve guests their first one and allow them to refill their own cup.

New Mexico Green Chili Stew with Chicken

There's really nothing else like a New Mexico Green Chili Stew. It's creamy without having cream, it's spicy without blowing your head off, and the depth and complexity of flavor is just off the charts delicious. I enjoy this soup served in a shallow bowl with a fried egg on top. Leave the yolk a little bit runny and then mix it into the soup and it becomes part of the broth!

Serves 12

- 2 tablespoons vegetable oil or canola oil
- 1 medium onion, diced
- 1-pound potatoes, preferably Idaho or Yukon gold, washed and cubed into ½-inch chunks
- 1-pound carrots, trimmed, washed and cut into ¼ inch slices or half-rounds
- 1 tablespoon minced garlic
- 2 teaspoons kosher salt
- ½ teaspoon freshly ground pepper
- ½ cup New Mexico green chilies, fire roasted, peeled, seeded and chopped.
- 2 teaspoons ground cumin
- 1 ½ teaspoons ground coriander
- ¾ cup flour
- 2 tablespoons dry vermouth
- 3 quarts chicken broth
- 2 cups canned hominy, rinsed and drained
- 2 cups frozen or fresh corn
- 2 ½ pounds cooked white meat chicken, cubed into ¾ -1 inch chunks
- 1 tablespoon fresh lime juice
- 1 cup chopped fresh cilantro

1. Put a large pot over medium heat on the stove. Add the chopped onions and cook until translucent. Then add the carrots, potatoes, garlic, salt, pepper, green chilies, cumin, coriander. Stir and cook until combined.
2. Add the flour and stir and cook until no white remains.
3. Add the dry vermouth and stir together until absorbed.
4. Add the chicken broth, hominy, and corn and cook simmering for 60 minutes until the potatoes and carrots are tender. Add the chicken and cook for 10 minutes to blend the flavors.
5. Add the lime juice and chopped cilantro, and taste for seasoning.
6. Add more salt, pepper, or lime juice to taste.

✎ NOTE:

Substitute the chicken with 2 ½ pounds of cooked, chopped pork. Add the pork after the carrots and potatoes are tender. Cook for an additional 15 minutes to blend the flavors.

Green Smoothie

I worked on this smoothie recipe for a few years. Once I had finally made something I loved, I started bottling it for the farmstand. Everyone loves this drink! My green smoothie recipe uses some superfood powder blends that I get online. There is no added sweetener, filler or preservative, it's loaded with vitamins, minerals, proteins and they are 100% organic.

Serves 12

- 2 pounds power greens- spinach, kale, Swiss chard
- 3 pounds frozen or fresh peaches, cleaned and pitted (peel on or off)
- 2 pounds frozen or fresh mangoes, cleaned and pitted (peel on or off)
- 4 large apples, cleaned and cored and chopped coarsely
- 12 – 20 cups water
- 4 cups apple cider (no sugar added)
- 1 cup protein powder blend (mine has pea protein, hemp protein, moringa, spirulina, alfalfa, rice protein, maca, lucuma and banana, and it has no sweetener or filler of any kind)
- ½ cup super-greens powder blend (mine has wheatgrass, barley grass, moringa, baobab, spirulina, and chlorella and it has no sweetener or filler of any kind)
- 1 bunch parsley
- ½ cup freshly squeezed lemon juice
- 3 large stalks celery, cleaned trimmed and chopped coarsely
- 2 large cucumbers, cleaned trimmed and chopped coarsely
- 3 bananas, peeled
- ¼ -½ cup maple syrup, start low and taste for sweetness. adjust as desired

1. In a blender (a serious blender that can really puree fruit and veggies. I have a BlendTec, and a Vitamix or equivalent would work here too), puree all ingredients in batches and add to a large bowl.
2. Taste and adjust maple syrup, water, and lemon juice to your personal taste and texture.

✎ NOTE:

Make a double batch, and package it in 12-ounce bottles. Freeze the bottles, and the smoothie stays fresh and bright green, until you are ready to drink it. Protein and super green powders can be purchased at yoursuper.com.

Chapter Four

Sides & Salads

These dishes can turn an ordinary meal into something really special or as an appetizer, set the stage for a remarkable experience. When you have an abundance of luscious summer garden tomatoes, Ratatouille and Panzanella can transform them into something transcendent! Garlic Soup soothes the body and soul, and Broccoli Cheese Soup is a warm and creamy vegetarian delight.

"I'm a great believer in luck, and I find the harder I work the more I have of it."

- THOMAS JEFFERSON

Sides & Salads

1. French Fries 101
2. Roasted Cauliflower 102
3. Ratatouille 103
4. Carrot Puree 105
5. Garlic Soup 106
6. California Slaw 107
7. Vinaigrette 109
8. Post Chuck E. Cheese Recovery Salad 110
9. Panzanella 112
10. Quinoa Salad 113
11. Pregnancy Salad 114
12. Celery Apple Salad 117
13. Broccoli Cheese Soup 118

French Fries

I think French fries might easily be one of my top 10 comfort foods. The addition of basic corn starch to the cooking fat leeches the moisture, allowing these fries to cook up nice and crispy, tender, moist and flavorful. Comfort food all the way.

Serves 1 per potato

- potatoes, standard Idaho potatoes are great
- extra virgin olive oil
- salt and pepper
- ½ teaspoon cornstarch

1. Preheat the oven to 400 degrees.
2. Clean and trim potatoes, and then cut into French fries. I typically cut the potato in half, pole to pole and then slice. Then cut the slices into fries.
3. Toss in a bowl with cornstarch and approximately 2 tablespoons of oil per potato.
4. Spread on a baking sheet and bake for 20 minutes or until crispy on the outside and tender on the inside.
5. Shake the pan or flip the potatoes' part way through cooking. About 20-30 minutes total is about right. This time can be adjusted down if you are using an air fryer or the convection setting on your oven.
6. Season to taste with salt and pepper and enjoy!

✎ NOTE:

Modify this recipe with duck fat and sweet potatoes.

Roasted Cauliflower

Roasting is a way to coax caramelization and sweetness from vegetables that most consider impossible. This roasted cauliflower is incredibly versatile! It's outstanding as an appetizer dipped in an aioli, as a side dish, with fried eggs and potatoes for breakfast, as a snack, and so much more.

Serves 4

- 1 large head of cauliflower, cleaned, trimmed, and chopped into small chunks, about an inch across or less.
- extra virgin olive oil to taste, but probably about 2 tablespoons
- salt and pepper to taste

1. Preheat the oven to 500 degrees. Line a cookie sheet with foil and spray with non-stick spray.
2. Spread cauliflower in an even layer, and drizzle with olive oil
3. Season with salt and pepper and bake on the top rack of the oven until tender, golden and caramelized on the edges, about 10-15 minutes, or more if needed.
4. Serve hot, warm or even at room temperature.

NOTE:

Other vegetables for roasting are carrots, parsnips, green beans, asparagus, onions, broccoli, and brussels sprouts.

Ratatouille

There is no better way to enjoy the fruits of a burgeoning summer garden than in Ratatouille. As such, make ratatouille only when you can get your hands on great tomatoes that have lots of fresh flavor. My favorite ways to enjoy ratatouille are as a side dish salad with a meal. As a condiment with eggs or lamb.

Serves 6

- 2 large eggplants
- kosher salt
- 2 red peppers
- 2 yellow peppers
- about 1/2 cup olive oil, for cooking
- 4 small zucchinis, cut into thick rounds
- 2 onions, sliced
- 2 cloves garlic, minced
- 2 pepperoncini peppers from a jar, crushed or minced very fine
- 1 bay leaf
- 1 sprig fresh rosemary
- 8 large tomatoes, seeded and roughly chopped
- freshly ground black pepper
- handful or 2 of chopped fresh basil leaves

1. Preheat the oven to broil. Thickly slice the eggplant and lay the rounds on cake racks which you've placed in the sink.
2. Salt, very generously, and leave 30 minutes for the excess water to drain off.
3. When they are ready, rinse them well under the tap and pat them dry with a towel.
4. While the eggplant drains, put the red and yellow peppers in the oven and broil to blacken the skin on all sides, 20 minutes total.
5. Remove to a bowl, cover with plastic wrap, and let sit for 5 minutes. The skin will now peel off easily. Peel and seed, then slice the flesh to julienne and put it in a large bowl.
6. Turn the oven down to 450 degrees. Put some oil on a baking sheet and toss the zucchini slices in it. "Grill" in the oven for 10 minutes, turning once.
7. Remove and add to the peppers.
8. Cut the rinsed and dried eggplant into large chunks, toss in oil, and spread on the baking sheet, and "grill" also, about 15 minutes.
9. As things are done add them to the bowl.
10. While the vegetables are in the oven, heat a spoonful of olive oil in a saute pan, and fry the onions until soft. Add the garlic, pepperoncini, bay leaf, and rosemary, and saute 1 minute.
11. Add the tomatoes. Cook the tomatoes until they are very soft and the whole mixture becomes thick and soupy, about 15 minutes.
12. Pour the tomato mixture over the vegetables and toss everything together. Check the seasonings to taste.
13. Serve at room temperature with the basil scattered over.

Carrot Puree

A staple at Thanksgiving dinner and any meal that includes lamb, carrot puree has been a family favorite for decades. Making sure the carrots are totally soft after cooking is critical to this recipe working. They must be soft enough to puree with the butter in the food processor, and if they are too hard, the vegetable puree will not be smooth.

Serves 4

- 2 pounds carrots, cleaned, trimmed and chopped coarsely into 1 ½ inch chunks
- 1 stick (8 tablespoons) butter, at room temperature
- ½ teaspoon salt

1. Boil a pot of salted water. Add the carrots and simmer until soft, about 20 minutes, but it could be longer.
2. Drain, and while the carrots are still warm, add them to the food processor and puree with the butter until smooth. Salt to taste and serve.

NOTE:

This dish reheats easily in the microwave, so it's a great one to make ahead of time.

Garlic Soup

Don't be intimidated by the large amount of garlic in this recipe. The cooking process produces an incredibly mild and sweet flavor from it, and it really is wonderful, especially on a cold night or when you are a little under the weather.

Serves 4

- 1 head garlic broken into cloves
- 5 teaspoons olive oil
- 4 large slices of focaccia bread, or country bread, not sourdough as it will make the soup sour. The slices should be large enough to span the width of your bowl without hanging over the edges.
- 1 teaspoon smoked paprika
- ½ teaspoon ground cumin
- 1 quart chicken broth or water
- 4 eggs

1. In a medium pot over medium heat, lightly brown the garlic in olive oil.
2. Remove the garlic from the pot with a slotted spoon and brown the bread slices on each side in the same pot.
3. Take the bread out and set aside. Sprinkle the bottom of the hot pot with paprika and cumin. Return the garlic to the pot along with the broth. Cover the pot and simmer until the garlic cloves soften, about 30 minutes.
4. Strain the soup through the finest disk of a food mill or puree it in a blender and strain it through a medium mesh strainer.
5. Preheat the oven to 350 degrees.
6. Bring soup back to simmer and ladle it into oven-proof bowls or soup crocks.
7. Place a browned bread slice on top of each one, then break an egg into each bowl on top of the bread.
8. Bake the soup until the egg white sets but the yoke is still runny; start checking after about six minutes.

California Slaw

This fresh, crispy tangy slaw is addictively delicious and can stand alone or be served with just about anything. I also love it with fried chicken, mushroom and black bean burgers, fresh fish and the yummiest Crispy Chinese Roasted Duck. See the recipe in the Fancy Pants chapter!

Serves 10

- 1 pound Napa cabbage, shredded
- 10 ounces snow peas thinly sliced
- 1 ½ cups radishes, thinly sliced
- 1 ½ cups scallions, thinly sliced
- 1 cup cilantro, chopped
- 1 cup small cucumbers, sliced
- 1 1/3 pound bacon, cooked until crispy and then chopped or crumbled
- 1 cup almonds, toasted and chopped
- 1 cup toasted salted pumpkin seeds
- 1 avocado, sliced.

Dressing

- 1 cup mayonnaise
- 3 tablespoons sugar
- 3 tablespoons rice vinegar
- 1 tablespoon soy sauce
- 1 minced garlic clove
- 1 tablespoon minced fresh ginger
- ½ teaspoon sesame oil
- ¼ teaspoon cayenne pepper (up to 1/2 tsp if want a little more spice)

1. Shake all dressing ingredients in a jar until well blended.
2. Combine all ingredients, save the avocado, in a medium bowl and toss with dressing. Place avocados and warm Crispy Chinese Roasted Duck on top.

Vinaigrette

I have been sampling and creating interesting salad combinations and dressings for many years. This Vinaigrette is full of flavor and my absolute favorite!

Yield 1 Cup

- 1 tablespoon Herbes de Provence
- 1 garlic clove, peeled and minced
- 1 tablespoon minced shallots
- 1 tablespoon freshly squeezed lemon juice
- 1 tablespoon Dijon mustard
- 1 tablespoon honey
- 3 tablespoons white wine vinegar
- salt and pepper
- ¾ cup extra virgin olive oil

1. Put everything except the oil in a clean jar (I use an old mustard or olive jar) and shake well.
2. Add oil and shake again. Taste for seasoning and adjust to your preference.

Here are a few ways to modify this recipe.

3. Remove garlic or lemon or mustard
4. Replace white wine vinegar with any vinegar you like. One of my favorites is called Banyuls vinegar.
5. Replace Herbes de Provence with an herb blend of your choice. There are some spice companies that have some interesting herb blends.
6. Replace the shallots with dried minced onion.

Post Chuck E. Cheese Recovery Salad

(Belgium Endive Salad With Beets & Winter Fruit)

After having attended an utterly chaotic children's birthday party at Chuck E. Cheese, I craved a bit of sophistication on my plate. I had to counteract pizza and orange soda in both my body and my soul, and this is what was created. It was a deep sigh of happiness on my peaceful fork. This recipe makes a salad for one.

Serves 1

- 1 Belgian endive
- 2 mandarin oranges, cut into segments
- 2 fresh sweet kiwi, peeled and sliced
- ¼ cup very thinly sliced red onions
- 2 tablespoons cider vinegar
- 2-3 tablespoons tangy mustard vinaigrette (recipe below)
- 2-3 small roasted golden beets (recipe below)

1. Roast the beets by trimming the stems and rinsing. Place in a foil pouch and drizzle with olive oil and a couple of pinches of salt. Make sure the foil pouch is closed and airtight. Roast at 400° for 45 minutes or until tender.

2. If your beets are large, this will take an hour or if they are extra-large, an hour and 15 minutes.

3. Once cool enough to handle, peel the beets and discard the peels. The peels should just slip right off.

4. Cut into wedges and reserve.

5. Put the sliced red onions in a bowl and drizzle cider vinegar on top. Salt and pepper to taste and toss to coat. Let sit for 15 minutes. This will pickle them.

6. Cut the mandarins into segments. To do this, cut each end off so the flesh shows. Cut off the peels by placing the mandarin on one of the cut off ends and working your way down the outside. Discard the peels.

7. Holding the orange in your hand over a bowl, use a paring knife to cut each segment out from the membranes. At the end you should have a bunch of gorgeous orange segments in a bowl and a blob of juicy membranes in your hand.

8. Squeeze as much juice as you can out of the membranes and reserve.

9. Peel the endive leaves apart and arrange on a large plate or platter. Top with kiwi slices, pickled red onions, beet wedges and orange segments. Drizzle reserved mandarin orange juice on top and then drizzle vinaigrette on top. Enjoy!

Tangy Mustard Vinaigrette

- 1 tablespoon Herbes de Provence
- 1 garlic clove, peeled and
- 1 tablespoon minced shallots
- 1 tablespoon freshly squeezed lemon juice
- 1 tablespoon Dijon mustard
- 1 tablespoon honey
- 3 tablespoons white wine vinegar
- salt and pepper
- ¾ cups extra virgin Olive Oil

1. Put everything except the oil in a clean jar (I use an old mustard or olive jar) and shake well.
2. Add oil and shake again.
3. Taste for seasoning and adjust to your preference.

Panzanella

The main keys to this salad being incredible are the freshness of the ingredients, especially the tomatoes, and the quality of the bread. In the summer, when garden tomatoes are plump, juicy, sweet and a lovely color of red is when its best to make this!

Makes a lot

- 10 pounds of really great summer tomatoes. If they are not great don't make this salad. Feel free to use a variety of different tomatoes here, or all the same kind.
- ¾ cup olive oil
- ¼ cup red wine vinegar
- 1 loaf crusty Italian bread, like a tuscan boule or a ciabatta. Don't use sourdough, it will severely impact the flavor of this salad, and it destroys the freshness of it!
- 1-2 stalks celery (or 3-4 small ones), chopped
- 1 bell pepper, chopped
- 1 red onion, chopped, and then let it sit in a bowl of water for about 10-15 minutes, drain and discard the water. This will remove the sharpness of the onion flavor.
- fresh basil, chopped
- fresh oregano, chopped
- salt and pepper to taste

1. Cut bread into ½-inch to 1-inch cubes and spread them on a cookie sheet to lightly toast in a 350 F oven for 5-10 minutes, turning once, until they are slightly crisp on the outside but still soft and pliable.
2. Once lightly toasted, put all the bread in a big bowl.
3. Chop tomatoes and put them and their juice on top of the bread. Tomatoes go first so that their juice is the first thing to soak into the bread.
4. Add olive oil and vinegar and toss. The order here is important, as you want the bread to absorb the flavor in the juice from the tomatoes first, then the oil, then the vinegar.
5. Chop the celery, bell pepper, onion, basil and oregano and add the salad.
6. Toss, season with salt and pepper, and serve within a few hours.

NOTE:

Optional add-ins, pitted chopped olives of any kind, chopped cucumbers, chopped scallions and/or chives, a very good can of tuna or salmon in olive oil, rinsed and drained canned cannellini beans, sun dried tomatoes, pumpkin seeds, or whatever else you can dream up!

Quinoa Salad

This quinoa salad is amazing and flexible. Not only can you add your favorite ingredients to customize it, but it is also delicious in many applications. My favorites are as a side dish, an ingredient in any kind of a wrap or sandwich, or an addition to a bunch of lettuce and dressing to make an automatically interesting and unique delicious salad.

Serves 6

- 1 ½ cups pecans, toasted and chopped
- 1 cup quinoa
- 3 small or 2 large ribs of celery, diced
- 3 small Persian or 1 large hothouse cucumber, chopped
- 1 cup loosely packed fresh arugula, rinsed, dried and chopped
- 1 can (15 ounces) garbanzo beans, rinsed and drained
- 1/3 cup extra-virgin olive oil
- 3 tablespoons freshly squeezed lemon juice (about 1-2 lemons)
- 2 teaspoons kosher salt
- ¼ teaspoon freshly ground black pepper

1. In a small pot with a lid, combine the quinoa with 2 cups of water and bring to a boil. Decrease the heat, cover and simmer until the water is absorbed, about 12-15 minutes.

2. Spread the quinoa on a large plate to cool.

3. Meanwhile combine all other ingredients in a large bowl, and then mix in the cooled quinoa. Refrigerate and enjoy at will!

Pregnancy Salad, a.k.a. Hot Summer Night Tuna Salad

This salad was born one evening when I was hot, pregnant and didn't feel like cooking. What I created was an amazing pasta and tuna salad dinner with an Asian flair. It is crispy with cabbage, creamy with mayonnaise and sesame oil and soy sauce, and flavorful with canned tuna in olive oil and sweet pickles or salty capers.

Serves 2

- 1 can of very good tuna fish packed in olive oil, drained
- 2 tablespoons your favorite relish or chopped capers
- 2/3 cups shredded cabbage
- 3 ounces pasta, your choice of shape, cooked, drained, and still warm
- ¼ cup mayonnaise
- 1 tablespoon soy sauce (or 2 teaspoons if you use capers)
- 1 teaspoon sesame oil

1. Cook and drain the pasta.
2. Meanwhile, mix all other ingredients gently so as not to break up the tuna too much.
3. Stir in the warm pasta, taste for seasoning, adjust as needed and enjoy.

✎ NOTE:

Don't let this sit too out long, as it is warm and has mayonnaise. Enjoy it right away or store it in the refrigerator to eat later.

Celery Apple Salad

This is a very fresh and crisp salad complemented by smoked almonds. The first time I made this salad was for Thanksgiving. I needed something that was fresh to go with all the mounds of deliciously rich food. It was such a nice addition to the feast that I have gone back and made it so many times since then. I just love it any time of the year!

Serves 4

- 1 head Romaine or Boston bib lettuce, roughly chopped or hand torn
- 2 stalks celery, sliced thin
- 1 green apple, quartered, cored and sliced thin
- smoked almonds, chopped
- fresh lemon juice from one lemon
- 2 teaspoons rice wine vinegar
- 3 tablespoons extra virgin Olive oil
- salt and pepper to taste

1. Rinse, dry and either rip or chop the lettuce into the bowl.
2. Toss in the celery, apple, and smoked almonds.
3. Whisk together the lemon juice, rice wine vinegar, olive oil, salt and pepper in a separate bowl or jar.
4. Dress with your preferred amount of dressing, toss and serve.

SIDES & SALADS

Broccoli Cheese Soup

This soup is insanely popular at my farmstand. The flavors from the vegetables, cheeses and spices are far greater together than their individual parts. I love it when that happens.

Serves 8

- 1 medium onion, chopped fine
- 1 stick (8 tablespoons) of butter
- 1 teaspoon kosher salt
- ¼ teaspoon fresh ground black pepper
- ¾ pound carrots, chopped coarsely
- 2/3 cup flour
- 3 small, or 2 medium-large heads of broccoli, chopped coarsely
- 1 quart (4 cups) of half and half
- 1 quart (4 cups) of chicken broth or vegetable broth
- 1 ½ teaspoons dried mustard
- 1 ½ teaspoons smoked paprika
- pinch of cayenne pepper
- 1 pound of cheddar cheese, shredded

1. Melt the butter in a large pot over low to medium heat.
2. Add onion, carrot, salt and pepper and cook until onion is slightly softened and translucent, about 5 minutes.
3. Add the flour, cook and stir until no white streaks remain, about a minute.
4. Add the half and half, broth, dried mustard, smoked paprika and cayenne and cook and whisk occasionally until smooth and cohesive, about 15 minutes.
5. Add the broccoli and cook until tender, about 15-20 minutes.
6. Remove from heat, slowly stir in the cheese until everything is blended, and taste for seasoning.
7. Add more salt, pepper and/or cayenne to taste.

NOTE:

Replace some of the cheddar with a little gruyere cheese and add a bacon crumble on top.

Chapter Five

Fancy Pants

You don't need to host a fancy dinner party to make these luscious and impressive meals, but you can confidently serve them to anyone if you do. All day Short Ribs that warm the soul, a Crab Omelet fit to ring in the new year, Filet Mignon with a sauce that makes diners do an involuntary sigh and this-is-so-delicious eye-roll, and even the best Italian Veal Osso Bucco will have you feeling like you just opened the best restaurant in town. Where will you start!?

"The truth is, you don't know what is going to happen tomorrow."

– EMINEM

Fancy Pants

1. Osso Buco 125
2. Filet Mignon with Bordelaise 127
3. Short Ribs 129
4. Crispy Chinese Roasted Duck 130
5. Crab Omelet 132
6. Quiche Lorraine 134
7. Oysters Adrienne 137
8. Escargots 138
9. Risotto 139
10. Artichokes 144
11. Composed Niçoise Salad 146
12. Chicken Bouillabaisse with Rouille 148
13. Beef Burgundy 151
14. Butterflied Leg of Lamb 153

Osso Buco

One of my most favorite and very dramatic meals is Osso Buco. Osso Buco is an Italian word which means bone with a hole, referring to the shank of a veal. This rich Osso Buco is full of soft flavorful vegetables, fresh pasta, and meat that is falling off the bone.

Serves 4

- 4 veal shanks, about 1 ½ to 2 inches thick
- salt and pepper
- 1/4 cup flour
- 2 tablespoons olive oil
- 2 tablespoons butter
- fresh herbs for a bouquet garni, which is a few sprigs of parsley and thyme and a bay leaf, tied with a bit of kitchen string. For dried herbs, use 1 teaspoon of each and place in a piece of cheesecloth, tied closed with kitchen string.
- 1 large onion, chopped
- 6-8 large carrots, chopped
- 4 stalks of celery, chopped
- 4 cloves of garlic, smashed
- 1 cup dry white wine
- 3 cups chicken stock

1. Preheat the oven to 350 degrees.
2. Generously salt and pepper the shanks, dredge them in the flour and then brown them in a large Dutch oven on medium to medium-high heat in which you have melted the butter and olive oil.
3. When they are golden brown on all sides, remove from the pot and set aside on a plate.
4. Put the onions, carrots and celery directly in the pot and cook until soft. If it seems a little dry, add a little splash more olive oil and a dab of butter.
5. Once the onions are soft, add the herb bouquet, wine and garlic and cook, scraping the brown yummy bits off the bottom of the pan with a wooden spoon, until the wine has mostly evaporated.
6. Put the veal and any juices from it back in the pot.
7. Add the chicken stock and cook in the oven for 2 ½ hours. When it's done the meat will be tender and fall off the bone and the sauce will smell seriously divine.
8. Serve over pasta, rice, bulgur, quinoa, or risotto. Make sure each person gets a shank and a couple spoons full of delectable sauce. Enjoy!

NOTE:

Any extra sauce can be used as an incredible pasta sauce or veggie drizzle.

SIDES & SALADS

Filet Mignon with Bordelaise

Although it can be hard to imagine a filet mignon that is perfectly cooked with salt and pepper tasting any better, I believe adding a bordelaise achieves just that! It's extra delicious! The way the sauce emulsifies when it all comes together makes the Filet Mignon velvety and rich.

Serves 4

- 4 filet mignon steaks
- 6-7 tablespoons butter, divided
- 4-5 scallions white and green parts, chopped
- ½ cup red wine
- salt and pepper to taste

1. Dry, salt and pepper the steaks.
2. Cook the steaks in a sauté pan in 1 tablespoon butter at medium high heat to medium rare or rare. If your steaks are 1 ½ inches thick, this usually takes me 2 ½ - 4 minutes per side.
3. Take the steaks out of the pan and pour out the grease. Reduce the heat to medium and add 1-2 tablespoons of butter and scallions.
4. Cook for about 5 minutes until onions become translucent.
5. Add ½ cup red wine and turn the burner to high heat. Deglaze the pan using a wooden spoon to scrape any brown bits from the bottom as cook the wine down until it's about ¼ of its original volume, about 2-4 minutes.
6. Remove the pan from heat. Using a silicone whisk, beat in 4 tablespoons of soft butter.
7. Taste for seasoning and add salt and pepper to your preference.
8. Serve immediately, spooning the sauce over the steak.

✎ NOTE:

To change the flavor profile, swap the red wine for a dry white wine like chardonnay, sauvignon Blanc or champagne.

Short Ribs

I think beef short ribs are one of the perfect foods to cook in a slow cooker. For this recipe, I combine Asian flavors; the soy sauce, ginger, scallions with some decidedly more European flavors; the garlic, Dijon mustard, with a splash of American flavors; the ketchup and brown sugar, for a version of short ribs that cooks all day, smells tangy and amazing and tastes even better! These ribs are a little sweet, a little spicy and very delicious. In fact, of all the meals I make, this is the most requested dinner item of all my friends and family!

Serves 4

- 4 pounds of boneless beef short ribs
- 1 cup soy sauce
- 1/3 cup of brown sugar or honey
- ¼ cup cider vinegar
- 2 cloves garlic, peeled and crushed
- 1 tablespoon grated fresh ginger
- ½ teaspoon crushed red pepper
- 1 teaspoon Tabasco
- 2-3 tablespoons Dijon mustard
- 1/3 cup ketchup
- 2 teaspoon dried minced onion
- 2 teaspoon dried oregano
- ½ teaspoon celery salt
- 2 tablespoons cornstarch
- 2 teaspoons sesame oil
- 3-4 scallions, thinly sliced (optional)

1. Mix all ingredients except the meat, cornstarch, sesame oil and scallions in a large measuring cup with a whisk.
2. Put the meat in the slow cooker and pour the sauce over it.
3. Cook on low for about 9-10 hours. I usually check partway through the cooking time to reposition the meat and make sure it all gets some time under the sauce.
4. Remove the meat from the slow cooker into a big bowl or onto a plate. It will be so tender, it should kind of fall apart.
5. Let the sauce settle for a few minutes and then spoon the visible fat off the top.
6. Whisk in the cornstarch, scallions and sesame oil and put some of the sauce over the meat. You can serve more on the side for dipping and drizzling over the meat.
7. Serve with pasta, rice, or just enjoy by themselves!

Crispy Chinese Roasted Duck

I borrowed ideas from a lot of different places and added quite a few of my own to pull this recipe together. There are a lot of cookbooks that recommend you steam a duck to render the fat before roasting it to get the crispy skin. This is a messy and cumbersome process. Then I read cookbook; My Father's Daughter: Delicious Easy Recipes Celebrating Family & Togetherness, by Gwyneth Paltrow. She recommends steaming it in the oven and I think it's brilliant! This is a simple, easy way to make a juicy, crispy flavorful duck!

Serves 6

- 1 large duck
- salt and pepper
- 1 small yellow onion, quartered
- 2 teaspoons Chinese 5-spice powder
- 2 tablespoons brown sugar

1. Preheat the oven to 350 degrees.
2. Trim the extra skin from the neck and back of the duck and remove the neck and any giblets inside.
3. Pierce the skin with the tip of a sharp knife (like a small paring knife) 50 to 60 times without piercing the meat.
4. Generously salt and pepper the bird inside and out.
5. Stuff with quartered onion. Sprinkle breast and back with five spice powder.
6. Place duck on a roasting rack inside a roasting pan and pour boiling water into the pan a half inch deep and add the brown sugar to the water.
7. Cover the entire pan with the duck in it with aluminum foil and seal tightly on the edges. Bake for one hour on each side for a total of 2 hours (flip the duck over and recover it halfway through cooking).
8. Cool the duck and then put on a plate, cover with foil, and refrigerate overnight.
9. Put the broth into a saucepan (or leave it in the roasting pan to do this) and simmer for about half an hour until it is reduced by half. Let it cool and cover it and refrigerate overnight as well.
10. Finish the duck the next day, by cooking it uncovered in a roasting pan on a rack at 500° degrees for 30 to 40 minutes, flipping it every 15 minutes, until the skin is crispy and brown.
11. Let it rest on a cutting board, covered with foil for about 10 minutes before carving into pieces. This will preserve the juiciness of the meat.
12. While the duck is resting, remove the fat from the top of the cold broth and discard. Warm the broth and use for moistening the meat.

✎ NOTE:

Reserve some meat to top the California Slaw. See the Sides & Salads chapter.

Crab Omelet

This dish is probably not like any other omelet you may have had. With a sour cream and wine-based filling it's pretty fancy, and is perfectly acceptable served as breakfast, brunch, or lunch!

Serves 4

Filling

- 2 cups sour cream
- 1/3 cup dry white wine or dry champagne
- 1 cup shredded cheddar cheese
- salt and pepper to taste
- 3 raw scallions, cleaned, trimmed and minced (both green and white parts)
- ½ pound cleaned crab, in ½ inch chunks or smaller
- 4 large slices of thick cut bacon, cooked until crispy

Wrap

- 2 tablespoons butter
- 8 large eggs
- ½ cup water
- salt and pepper

1. Combine the sour cream, wine, cheese, salt, pepper, and scallions in a medium bowl. GENTLY fold in the crab, so you don't break it up too much.
2. Cover and rest in the refrigerator for 1 hour or up to 8 hours.
3. Add 1 ½ teaspoons of butter to a 6 -7 inch skillet on medium heat.
4. While the butter melts, whisk 2 eggs in a bowl with 2 tablespoons of water.
5. Once the butter is melted and the pan is hot, swirl the butter around to coat the bottom of the pan and then add the eggs.
6. Cook, gently lifting the edge of the eggs to let some of the uncooked eggs slide around the pan. Don't mix or scramble the eggs once they are in the pan. You want them to stay smooth like a sheet so that you can wrap.
7. Once the eggs look firm on bottom (they should still be yellow and almost firm on the top), place ½ cup filling in a line down the center.
8. Place an entire slice of bacon on top of the filling.
9. Use a spatula to gently fold the sides around the filling and tip and roll the omelet onto a warm plate. I warm the plates by microwaving them empty for 30 seconds.
10. Add another ½ teaspoon of butter to the pan and repeat until all omelets are complete.

✎ NOTE:

You can replace the crab with cooked chopped shrimp, scallops or use all three!

Quiche Lorraine

Quiche Lorraine reminds me of my childhood Christmas mornings with my family. My mom would make the quiche, and my dad would rant and rave about how she could serve it in the "finest restaurant". My dad wasn't wrong, it was the most delicious of quiches I've ever had. This version of Quiche Lorraine is loaded with bacon, Gruyere cheese, heavy cream and eggs. The custard is tender and wonderful, and the pie can be served warm or at room temperature or even cold. It will basically wait for you- making it as easily suited to Christmas morning as it is for brunch, lunch, supper or dinner.

Serves 8

Crust

- 2 cups flour
- ½ cup cold butter, cut into 8-10 small pieces
- ½ cup cold vegetable shortening
- 2 teaspoon sugar
- ½ teaspoon kosher salt
- 8-12 tablespoons. ice water

Filling

- 10 slices thick bacon, cooked until crisp
- 2 cups shredded gruyere cheese
- 4 eggs yolks
- 4 whole eggs
- 1 ½ cups heavy cream
- 1 ½ cups milk
- 1 teaspoon kosher salt
- a pinch of black pepper
- 2 tablespoons butter

1. Preheat your oven to 400 degrees.
2. Combine flour, sugar, salt, butter and shortening in a bowl using 2 butter knives or a pastry blender until the butter and shortening are the size of small peas.
3. Add 8 tablespoons of ice water and mix in with a fork to form a ball. If it's too dry to form a ball, dribble in more ice water, 1 tablespoon at a time until it comes together.
4. Roll out on a floured surface and put into a greased 11-12 inch quiche pan and pinch the edges with your fingers to make a scalloped look.
5. Prick the bottom with a fork, cover with a buttered piece of parchment or foil, and top with pie weights.
6. Bake for 10 minutes.
7. Remove parchment and weights, prick with a fork again.
8. Bake for 3 more minutes, remove from the oven and turn the oven temperature down to 325 degrees.
9. Scatter the bacon and the cheese evenly on the bottom of the baked crust.
10. In a blender, whisk the eggs, yolks, milk, cream, salt and pepper.
11. Pour into the crust and dot the top of the unbaked pie with the butter.

12. Bake 45 minutes or until the top is golden in parts and the custard is just set.

13. Let it rest at least 20 minutes after coming out of the oven, no matter how yummy it looks and smells!

14. Serve warm, at room temperature or cold.

 NOTE:

The bacon can be swapped with a multitude of other ingredients. Some of the most popular flavors of quiche at the farmstand are

- spinach
- spinach and sauteed mushrooms
- green chilis, corn and Monterey jack cheese
- zucchini, corn, cherry tomatoes and basil (use mozzarella cheese)
- caramelized brussels sprouts and bacon
- roasted red peppers and broccoli

Just toss a small handful into the crust before adding the cheese and egg mixture.

Oysters Adrienne

This is a type of oyster stew that is creamy and spicy with a freshness from chopped parsley and shallots. Oysters are amazing in December, or generally in the winter months, they're fresh, sweet and salty like the sea.

Serves 6

- 1 pint (16 ounces) oysters, shucked
- ½ cup oyster water (juice from the oysters plus water to make 1/2 cup)
- ½ cup chopped shallots, minced, separate out 1-2 tablespoons and set aside
- ¼ cup parsley, chopped
- ½ cup dry white wine or dry champagne
- ¼ teaspoon ground black pepper
- ¼ cup butter
- 3 tablespoons flour
- ¾ cup half and half
- ½ teaspoon cayenne pepper, or more to taste
- salt to taste

1. In a shallow pan, poach the oysters in the oyster water with the ½ cup shallots, parsley, wine and black pepper.
2. Bring to a low boil and cook for 2-3 minutes until the oyster's edges curl.
3. Meanwhile, melt the butter with the flour and salt in a small skillet over medium heat, whisking until melted and lightly browned.
4. Whisk in half and half, salt and cayenne until slightly thickened.
5. Turn off the heat, gently whisk the cream into the oysters and taste for seasoning, making any necessary adjustments.
6. Serve in shallow bowls and sprinkle with a few pinches of raw shallot.

Escargot

I tried escargot on a dare from my dad, while I was in Paris, completely sure I was going to hate it. But I couldn't believe how delicious those little snails were! The texture was extremely tender, and the sauce was full of flavor.

Serves 6

- 1 stick butter, softened
- 2 small cloves garlic, peeled and minced
- 2 tablespoon minced fresh parsley
- 1 small shallot, peeled and minced
- 1 teaspoon salt
- ¼ teaspoon fresh ground black pepper
- 2 teaspoons dry white wine
- 1 teaspoon cognac
- 2 dozen canned giant snails (snails from Burgundy are the best)
- 1 crusty baguette, warmed

1. In a bowl, beat together all ingredients except the snails and the bread. Cover and refrigerate for at least 4 hours or overnight or freeze for up to 2 months.
2. Preheat the oven to 400 degrees. Add the butter into a baking dish that is good at holding the heat. My favorite is a 10 inch enameled cast iron pan or you can use a 9 to 10 inch square glass baking dish.
3. When the butter has barely melted, add the snails and put it back in the oven.
4. Cook for 10 minutes or until the butter sizzles and snails are nice and hot.
5. Serve immediately with the bread, dipping the bread in the sauce and topping with the snails.

Risotto

The process of making Risotto is not to be rushed. It takes 20 to 30 minutes at the stove, stirring intermittently. There are no shortcuts to this recipe, but once it's finished, the variations are endless. In our house we rarely eat risotto by itself. It typically accompanies a steak or other protein and pairs beautifully with long braised meats like short ribs, Osso buco or even pot roast.

Serves 4

- ½ yellow onion, diced
- 1 tablespoon olive oil
- salt and pepper to taste
- 1 cup arborio rice
- ½ cup white wine
- 2-3 ½ cups chicken broth, warm
- 2 tablespoons butter

1. Put a medium sized pot over medium heat on the stove top. Add olive oil and onion and sauté until the onion is soft and translucent.
2. Add the rice, salt, and pepper and sauté until the rice starts to look translucent on the edges. This should only take about a minute.
3. Add the white wine and stir periodically until most of the wine has absorbed into the rice.
4. Add chicken broth about half of a cup at a time and continue to cook, stirring periodically until the broth mostly absorbs.
5. Keep adding the chicken broth in half cup increments and stirring to absorb until the rice tastes slightly form (al dente) but mostly tender.
6. The amount of chicken broth will vary depending on your rice and your preference for tenderness. Once the amount of chicken broth that brings your desired tenderness has been achieved.
7. Turn the heat off and stir in two tablespoons of softened butter.
8. Taste for seasoning and adjust with salt and pepper as desired.

NOTE:

Arborio is the only rice for this recipe. If you are in Italy, or have access to Italian food, you can use Baldo, Carnaroli, Maratelli, Padano, Ribe, Roma and Vialone Nano.

Notes – 32 ways to make it your own

1. SAFFRON

Add a pinch of saffron with the first addition of chicken broth and ½ cup grated parmesan cheese with the butter.

2. SAFFRON & PEAS

Add half cup frozen peas when the saffron risotto is done cooking.'

3. PORCINI MUSHROOM

Add an amber ale or your favorite beer (hoppy beers won't work here, go for an ale or lager) in the place of the wine and then add Porcini mushrooms (dried mushrooms, rinsed to remove grit) with the second addition of chicken broth

4. BUTTERNUT SQUASH

Add peeled, cubed ½ inch chunks of butternut squash with the onions and replace the chicken broth with vegetable broth

5. CAPRESE

Cube and sauté until softened and golden on the edges a small to medium stick of zucchini and ½ cup of halved grape tomatoes. Add a few leaves of fresh shredded basil at the end of cooking and cook on low until warmed through. Top with cubed fresh mozzarella cheese and serve.

6. SHRIMP

Add ½ pound chopped cleaned raw shrimp with the last ½ cup chicken broth and cook until pink. Add 2 teaspoons lemon juice and 1 tablespoon drained capers with the butter and warm through.

7. LOBSTER

Gently fold in ½ pound cooked cleaned lobster chunks and 2 teaspoons lemon juice with the butter and warm through.

8. CRAB

Gently fold in ½ pound cooked cleaned crab, 2 teaspoons lemon juice, and 2 chopped scallions (both white and green parts) with the butter and warm through.

9. HENRY'S MEATY RISOTTO

With the onions, cook ½ pound ground beef, ½ pound Italian sausage (remove from casing and break apart), 1 tablespoon minced raw garlic and 1 cup frozen lima beans. Drain most of the fat before adding the risotto to the pan.

10. CORN & BACON

Add one cup frozen or fresh corn kernels and ¼ cup cooked crumbled bacon with the butter and warm through.

11. GREEN CHILI

Replace the white wine with 2 tablespoons of dry vermouth. Add one 4 ounce can drained, chopped green chilies with the butter and warm through.

12. SPINACH

Add 2 cups of washed dried baby spinach leaves and a pinch of nutmeg with the butter and heat until spinach wilts and warms through.

13. RISI BISI RISOTTO

Add 1 teaspoon minced garlic and 2 tablespoons chopped pancetta with the onions. With the butter, add 1 cup frozen petite peas, ½ cup grated parmesan, 2 tablespoons minced fresh parsley and 1 teaspoon lemon juice. Warm though.

14. THANKSGIVING

With the onions, add 1 cup chopped fresh green beans, ½ teaspoon dried thyme, 1 teaspoon minced fresh rosemary, ½ cup diced sweet potatoes and 3 tablespoons dried cranberries.

15. CARROT

With the onion, add ½ cup finely diced fresh carrot.

16. TARRAGON

After cooking, top risotto with 1-2 tablespoons of fresh tarragon, chopped or snipped.

17. FENNEL

Add a pinch of saffron and ½ cup cleaned, trimmed, chopped raw fennel (only the ribs) with the onions.

18. BACON & PEAS

At the end of cooking, add 1 cup frozen petite peas and ¼ cup chopped cooked crispy bacon. Warm through.

19. CARBONARA

At the end of cooking, add ½ cup grated parmesan, 1 teaspoon freshly ground black pepper, 2 tablespoons cream, and ¼ cup chopped, cooked crispy pancetta. Warm through.

20. BROCCOLINI & ROASTED RED PEPPERS:

With the onions, add 1 cup cleaned, trimmed, chopped fresh broccolini. At the end of cooking, add 3 tablespoons chopped roasted red peppers. Warm through. Top with ½ cup freshly grated parmesan cheese.

21. PROSCIUTTO & BRIE

With the butter, fold in ¼ cup prosciutto, chopped fine, and ¼ cup diced Brie cheese.

22. CAULIFLOWER & RAISINS with CURRY

With the onions, add 1 cup chopped raw cauliflower, 1 tablespoon curry, and 2 tablespoons raisins.

23. BROCCOLI & CHEDDAR

With the onions, add 1 cup cleaned, trimmed, chopped fresh broccoli. At the end of cooking, top with ½ cup grated cheddar cheese.

24. HAVARTI & DILL

At the end of cooking, top with ½ cup grated Havarti cheese and 3 tablespoons chopped fresh dill fronds.

25. BLUE CHEESE & BACON

At the end of cooking, top with 1/3 cup crumbled blue cheese and ¼ cup chopped cooked crispy bacon. Fold in gently (an outstanding side with prime rib).

26. KALE & CHEESE

With the onions, add 4 cups shredded kale. With the butter, add ¼ cup ricotta cheese, 2 tablespoons cream, ¼ cup grated parmesan, and ½ cup grated mozzarella cheese.

27. ANDOUILLE & DATES

With the onions, add ½ pound chopped (cooked / cured) andouille sausage and ½ cup chopped pitted dried dates. At the end of cooking, top with ½ cup grated cheese (Manchego, pecorino, or parmesan).

28. CARAMELIZED PEARL ONIONS & MUSHROOMS

In a separate pan while the risotto is cooking, put ½ stick butter (4 tablespoons), ½ package frozen peeled pearl onions (a full package is 14 ounces, so use about 7 ounces for this), 7 ounces cremini mushrooms (also called baby bella mushrooms), cleaned and sliced, and ½ teaspoon kosher salt in a skillet over medium high heat. Cook, stirring very little, until the mushrooms and onions are golden in parts. Remove from the heat, add 2 teaspoons lemon juice with the last ladle of chicken broth, add to the risotto and then finish cooking the risotto.

29. SUGAR SNAP PEAS -

Slice 1 cup fresh cleaned sugar snap peas into ½ inch pieces (cut crosswise). Sauté with 2 teaspoons extra virgin olive oil and ½ teaspoon salt separate from the risotto in a medium skillet over medium heat until just tender. With the butter, add sugar snaps snaps and warm through.

30. ONIONS & THYME -

In a separate pan while the risotto is cooking, put 1 tablespoon extra-virgin olive oil, one medium yellow onion, cleaned, peeled and sliced in ¼ inch thick slices cut top to bottom (think of the onion like a planet earth, and cut the slices from the north to south poles), ½ teaspoon thyme, ½ cup water, and 1 teaspoon salt. Cook over medium high heat, stirring periodically, until the onions caramelize and are golden. Add everything to the risotto with the butter and warm through.

31. LEMON & PARMESAN:

With the butter, add the zest and juice of one lemon and stir together until warm. Top with ½ cup grated parmesan cheese.

32. YOUR FAVORITE IDEA:

Your opportunity to make your own!

Artichokes

When it's artichoke season, I get a little giddy! What an awkward thing artichokes are to cook and eat but WOW so delightful. I've been enjoying artichokes prepared this way since I was very young. I love them just as much today as I did back then, thanks Mom!

Serves 4

- 4 whole fresh artichokes, trimmed, cut the very top off to flatten, peel off the super tough 3-4 outer leaves, and trim off the toughest part of the stem. Leave most of the stem on though, it is delicious
- 1 lemon, cut in half
- 2 cloves garlic, crushed
- 2 teaspoons dried Italian seasoning

1. Put a steamer basket and an inch or so of water in a large pot with a lid.
2. Bring to a boil, add the artichokes and immediately squeeze all the juice from the lemon on them so they don't turn brown.
3. Throw the lemon husks, garlic and Italian seasoning into the pot, cover, and steam about an hour until tender or when a knife easily pierces the stem.
4. Remove artichokes to a serving platter and serve with sauce.

Artichoke Dipping Sauce

- 3/4 cup mayonnaise
- juice of one lemon
- 1-2 cloves of garlic, crushed (to your taste)

1. Mix ingredients, taste for seasoning and adjust any of the ingredients to your liking. Serve with cooked artichokes.

FANCY PANTS

Composed Niçoise Salad

My friend Susan turned me on to the Niçoise salad and I learned that it was something I could make at home versus only having in a French restaurant. The key to this wonderful salad is getting the right ingredients. Building it and putting it together is almost an art. Enjoy it for lunch or dinner.

Serves 2

- 3 cups green beans, French green beans are best (haricots vert) steamed/boiled for 5 minutes or until just tender and then cooled/chilled
- 3 tomatoes quartered, or a dozen + cherry or grape tomatoes
- 1 cup vinaigrette (see recipe below)
- 1 head of butter/Boston lettuce washed and dried
- 3 cups cold French potato salad (see recipe below)
- ½ cup Niçoise olives pitted or kalamata olives
- 3 hard-boiled eggs, cold, peeled, quartered lengthwise
- 12 anchovy filets drained
- 1 can good tuna, oil packed (Italian or Spanish is the best)
- 2-3 tablespoons capers
- ½ cup flat leaf parsley, chopped, divided (part goes in the potatoes and part get sprinkled over the whole thing)
- 1 large platter

Tangy Mustard Vinaigrette

- 1 tablespoon Herbes de Provence
- 1 garlic clove, peeled and minced
- 1 tablespoon minced shallots
- 1 tablespoon freshly squeezed lemon juice
- 1 tablespoon Dijon mustard
- 1 tablespoon honey
- 3 tablespoons white wine vinegar
- salt and pepper
- ¾ cup extra virgin olive oil

1. Put everything except the oil in a clean jar (I use an old mustard or olive jar) and shake well.
2. Add oil and shake again.
3. Taste for seasoning and adjust to your preference.

French potato salad

- 1-pound small red potatoes
- 1 tablespoon dry vermouth
- ¼ cup vinaigrette
- 1 tablespoon minced shallots or scallions
- 2 tablespoons minced parsley

1. Boil the potatoes in salted water unpeeled until tender.
2. Slice into quarters (halves depending upon size) while warm.

3. Toss with the vermouth and let it soak in a few minutes. T

4. Toss with the vinaigrette and let soak in.

5. Add shallots & parsley.

Build the Salad

1. Toss the lettuce leaves with ¼ cup of vinaigrette and place around the platter.

2. Arrange each item in a pile, on top of the lettuce leaves in sections.

3. Sprinkle w/ chopped parsley.

4. Just before serving, season green beans and tomato wedges with several spoons full of dressing.

Chicken Bouillabaisse with Rouille

From my recipe tester friend, Cynthia Ellington, owner of culinary business, 'Cynfully Delicious' -

"The Bouillabaisse and Rouille were spot on delicious! This recipe was surprisingly easy but tastes like it took hours and a culinary degree to complete. I truly love that anyone at any level of cooking can do this. This is definitely in the family meal rotation and makes me wish it was still winter so I could eat it every day. This Rouille...is aioli on crack times two! You weren't kidding about wanting to put it on everything😂🤭 this is going to be my new veggie dip, sandwich spread, maybe use in place of hollandaise on my eggs...I will make stuff up to put it on."

This addiction-worthy chicken recipe is incredible on its own and especially amazing served with fresh crusty bread.

Serves 4

- 3 pounds of bone-in, skin-on thighs and legs or split breasts cut in half
- salt and pepper
- 2 tablespoons extra virgin olive oil
- 2 large onions, peeled and chopped
- 4 garlic cloves, minced
- 2 tablespoons tomato paste
- 2 tablespoons flour
- ¼ teaspoon saffron threads, crumbled
- ¼ teaspoon cayenne pepper
- 1 tablespoon smoked paprika
- 1 tablespoon fennel seeds, 1 teaspoon kosher salt and 1 tablespoon dried rosemary, ground in the spice grinder
- 4 cups chicken broth
- 3 large tomatoes, cored and chopped, or one 14.5-ounce canned diced tomatoes
- 1 pound Yukon gold potatoes, cut into ¾ inch pieces
- ¾ cup dry white wine
- 1 3-inch strip of orange zest
- crusty bread (I recommend the plain focaccia recipe in this book)
- Rouille (see recipe below)

1. Heat oven to 375 degrees. Pat chicken pieces dry with paper towels and season generously with salt and pepper.

2. Heat oil in a Dutch oven over medium high heat until just smoking.

3. Brown chicken well, 5-8 minutes per side and then transfer to plate.

4. Add onion to fat left in the pot and cook, stirring often, until beginning to soften and turn translucent, about 5 minutes.

5. Stir in garlic, tomato paste, flour, saffron, cayenne, smoked paprika, and fennel-salt-rosemary blend and cook until fragrant, about 30 seconds.

6. Slowly whisk in broth while scraping up any browned bits and smoothing out any lumps.

7. Stir in tomatoes, potatoes, wine and orange zest. Bring to a simmer and cook for 10 minutes.

8. Nestle the chicken pieces into the pot, keeping the skin above the surface of the liquid. Cook in the oven uncovered, for 30 minutes.

9. Remove the pot from the oven. Using a large spoon, skin the excess fat from the surface of the stew.

10. Season with salt and pepper to taste. Serve in wide shallow bowls with fresh crusty bread and rouille. I like to drizzle the rouille all over the soup (which enhances the broth) AND the bread (which I made into the soup).

Rouille

- ¼ cup boiling water
- ¼ teaspoon saffron threads, crumbled
- 1 slice plain white bread, broken into small pieces
- 1 ½ tablespoons lemon juice (freshly squeezed)
- 2 egg yolks
- 1 tablespoon Dijon mustard
- 3 small garlic cloves, minced
- ¼ teaspoon cayenne pepper
- 1 ¼ cups regular olive oil

1. Crumble saffron into the food processor and pour boiling water over it. Let steep for 5 minutes.

2. Sprinkle the bread into the saffron water along with the lemon juice.

3. Pulse until blended. Add egg yolks, mustard, garlic, and cayenne and pulse again until blended.

4. Put the lid on the processor, turn on and SLOWLY pour in oil as mixture emulsifies.

5. When all the oil is incorporated it should look like bright yellow mayonnaise.

6. Season to taste with salt and pepper. Don't be surprised if you want to put it on everything!

Beef Burgundy

If you like beef and have never had real French Beef Burgundy, also known as "Boef Bourguignon", then you are going to fall in love! The beef is so incredibly tender, and the flavor is so deep and primal, it's no wonder it was one of Julia Child's most famous signature dishes. The vegetables in this recipe can easily be increased, but if you swap vegetables, you can expect a different flavor profile. The long cooking process and browning steps mean that every single vegetable and spice plays an important role in the symphony of flavors. You will want a large Dutch oven (mine is enameled cast iron, and if you don't have one, it's a great investment for the serious cook) for this recipe, that is both stovetop and oven safe. It's a recipe that braises for a while and a nice heavy pot helps the process.

Serves 10

- 4 pounds beef, cut into 1-inch chunks
- 1 ½ cups flour
- salt and pepper
- 3 tablespoons extra virgin olive oil, plus more if needed
- 4 tablespoons butter, plus more (see below)
- 3 slices thick bacon, chopped
- ½ cup water
- 2 tablespoons brandy
- ¾ pound carrots, trimmed and cleaned and chopped into ½ inch chunks
- 1 medium yellow onion, diced
- 1 pound Yukon gold or russet potatoes, scrubbed and chopped into ¾ inch chunks (slightly larger than the carrots)
- 1-2 turnips, trimmed and cleaned and chopped into ½ inch chunks
- 1 bunch parsley, chopped (stems and leaves) fine
- 1 bay leaf
- ½ teaspoon dried thyme
- 2 quarts chicken broth
- 1 bottle red wine (burgundy, cabernet, rioja, zinfandel, malbec, something full bodied that you would drink, but not your fanciest bottle)
- ½ pound mushrooms, preferably cremini (also known as baby bella), sliced
- 4 more tablespoons butter
- 1 6-ounce package of frozen pearl onions
- juice of 1 lemon

1. Preheat the oven to 350 degrees, about 15 minutes before you put the beef burgundy into the oven.

2. Place a large heavy pot that can also go into the oven (and has a lid) on the stove top at medium heat. Add the extra virgin olive oil and 4 tablespoons butter and heat until melted but not burned.

3. Meanwhile, place the flour, 2 teaspoons salt and 1 teaspoon pepper into a large zip top bag.

4. Dry the beef with paper towels and shake it in the seasoned flour.

5. Cook in the large pot only a few pieces of beef at time until golden brown on all sides, about 3-7 minutes per batch. As each piece becomes golden brown, set aside on a plate for later use.

6. Once all the beef is browned and set aside, turn the burner to medium-low and add the bacon to the pan. Cook the bacon until crispy.

7. Pour the water into the pan and use a wooden spoon to scrape the brown goodness off the bottom of the pan. This is where the deep complex flavor comes from in this dish, don't skip this step.

8. If the pan seems dry, add another tablespoon of oil, then add the carrots, onions, potatoes, turnips, and brandy.

9. Cook vegetables until slightly softened and the onions are translucent.

10. Add the parsley, bay leaf, thyme, chicken broth, red wine, salt and pepper and cook stirring occasionally until it comes to simmer.

11. Put the lid on, put it in the oven and cook for 3 hours.

12. Meanwhile put the additional 4 tablespoons butter in a saucepan at medium high heat.

13. Add mushrooms, salt and pepper and cook until the mushrooms are softened.

14. Add the pearl onions and continue to cook, stirring very little, until the mushrooms and onions are golden brown on the edges.

15. Remove from heat, add the juice of one lemon and stir.

16. Set aside until the pot comes out of the oven.

17. After the stew has cooked for 3 hours, remove the pot from the oven.

18. Carefully remove the lid, stir in the mushroom and onion mixture, and replace the lid and put the pot back into the oven for 30 more minutes.

19. Then remove from the oven and let the stew rest for 30 minutes. Remove the bay leaf.

20. Serve on its own in a shallow bowl or with pasta, potatoes, or rice. It's also lovely with spaghetti squash on the side.

NOTE:

For the beef, you can use stew meat, or you can buy a roast and cut it into 1-inch cubes. Use what looks best at the market.

Butterflied Leg of Lamb

In our house, there are a few things that Julia Child is best known for; fresh hollandaise sauce, potato leek soup and butterflied leg of lamb. My recipe is an adaptation of hers. This lamb is tender and flavorful, with a pink interior and a gorgeous flavor of rosemary, garlic, lemon and Dijon mustard. It is a favorite with every one of family members, and it is incredibly impressive as a dinner party or cocktail party offering.

Serves 4-8

- 1 leg of lamb, butterflied, trimmed, and cut into large lobes 2 ½ – 4 pounds
- 3 cloves garlic, crushed
- 2 teaspoon kosher salt
- 2 sprigs of fresh rosemary, de-stemmed, leaves snipped
- 1 ½ tablespoons Dijon mustard
- 2 tablespoons lemon juice, from about 1 lemon
- 2 tablespoons soy sauce
- ½ cup olive oil

1. Put the trimmed lamb into a large zipper bag.
2. Add all remaining ingredients except the olive oil to a clean glass jar. Shake well. Add olive oil, shake well again.
3. Pour over the meat, close the bag and place in the refrigerator to marinade for 2 hours or overnight.
4. Turn oven to 450 degrees. Remove meat from the bag and place on a cookie sheet. If your cookie sheet is not nonstick, you may want to line it with foil.
5. Cook for about 9-12 minutes on the top rack, which may vary from rare to medium, depending on the size of the pieces.
6. Remove from the oven, cover with foil and let rest for about 10 minutes or so.
7. Move to a cutting board and slice against the grain. Serve and enjoy!

Chapter Six

Sweets Upon Sweets

Whether you want to impress your guests at a party or start the ultimate dessert tradition, there's no denying that a wonderful dessert can create the most tender and happy memories. Wander through these pages to bake the best flaky pie crust, the most impressive chocolate desserts, and the keto sweets of your dreams.

"Be yourself; everyone else is already taken."

— OSCAR WILDE

Sweets Upon Sweets

1. Pie Crust & Nectarine Pie 158
2. German Chocolate Cupcakes 160
3. Carrot Cake Cupcakes 162
4. Brown Butter Bourbon Pecan Pie 164
5. Custard & Custard Pie 166
6. Green Tea Ice Cream 169
7. Salted Caramel 170
8. Salted Chocolate Chip Cookies (gluten free, vegan) 173
9. Peanut Butter Toffee 174
10. Flourless Chocolate Cake 176
11. Pots de Crème 179
12. Spiced Pear Custard Brulé Pie 180
13. Cheesecake 183
14. French Silk pie 185
15. Lemon Bars 186
16. Keto Lemon Bars 187
17. Lemon Lemon Cupcakes 188
18. Keto Pumpkin Bars 190
19. Keto Cheesecake 191
20. Chocolate Whiskey Cupcakes with Whiskey Caramel Frosting GF 193

Pie Crust & Nectarine Pie

There is something gloriously cathartic about making a fresh pie and crust. My grandmother taught me to make pie crust when I was very young and I've been making it for as long as I can remember. This is that same recipe, with a few little tweaks. It's perfect for sweet or savory pie!

Serves 6

Pie Crust

- 2 cups flour
- 2 teaspoons sugar
- 1 teaspoon salt
- ¼ cup butter, cold and cut into pieces (½ stick)
- ½ cup shortening
- 8-12 tablespoons ice water

1. Mix flour, sugar and salt in a bowl.
2. Add butter and shortening and mix in with a pastry blender or 2 butter knives until the butter and shortening pieces are about the size of small peas. NO SMALLER or the crust will be dry and tough.
3. Add 8 tablespoons of ice water and mix in with a fork. If the dough does not come together in a ball, mix in up to 2 more tablespoons of ice water.
4. Shape dough into a ball, cover with plastic wrap, and put in the refrigerator for at least 30 minutes (colder is better here). This can be done up to 2 days before use.

Nectarine Pie

- 3 ½ pounds nectarines cut into chunks – do not peel
- you can replace up to 1 pound of the nectarines with peaches, plums, pluots, blackberries, blueberries, or raspberries without adjusting the rest of the recipe
- zest and juice of 1 lime
- 1 cup plus 2 tablespoons sugar
- 3 tablespoons tapioca
- 3 tablespoons flour

1. Preheat the oven to 450 degrees. Mix cleaned and cut up fruit, lime zest and juice, and 1 cup of sugar together in a bowl.
2. Put remaining 2 tablespoons sugar, tapioca and flour into a spice grinder / coffee grinder and grind together until fine.
3. Add to fruit bowl and mix in.
4. Cover bowl with plastic wrap, and let it sit on the counter so the flavors can develop, and the fruit can sweeten and plump for about an hour.
5. Remove dough ball from refrigerator and cut in half. Roll each piece on a floured cold surface (like the kitchen counter) into a large circle that fits in your (approximately 10-inch) pie plate with about 2-3 inches of an overhang.
6. Gently push the crust into the corners of the pan.
7. Add filling, add top crust, cut vents in top crust and the crimp edges closed with a fork or your fingers.
8. Sprinkle the top with sugar. (for a shiny pie, brush with a whisked egg white before you sprinkle with the sugar)
9. Bake for 25 minutes until the top is golden.
10. Reduce the temperature to 375 degrees and continue baking for another 25-30 minutes until the filling is bubbly.
11. Let cool at least an hour before serving.

German Chocolate Cupcakes

My Dad's birthday cake, every year was German Chocolate. By the time he reached his 70's his favorite became these German Chocolate cupcakes. They are the perfect size to enjoy and have a cult-like following at my farmstand.

Makes 24

- 2 ½ cups flour
- ½ cup cocoa powder
- 1 cup espresso americano or good coffee
- 1 cup sour cream
- 4 teaspoons vanilla
- 24 tablespoons (3 sticks) unsalted butter, softened but still cool
- 2 ½ cups sugar
- 6 eggs, room temp
- 1 teaspoon baking soda
- 1 teaspoon salt

Coconut-Pecan Filling

- 8 large egg yolks
- 2 cups sugar
- ½ teaspoon salt
- 16 tablespoons (2 sticks) unsalted butter, softened but still cool
- 2 cups heavy cream
- 2 teaspoons vanilla
- 3 cups chopped pecans, toasted
- 4 cups lightly packed sweetened flaked coconut, lightly toasted. Toast in a dry pan over low heat or in the oven at 350 on a cookie sheet for about 5 minutes.

1. Preheat oven to 350 degrees. Line a 24-capacity muffin tin with cupcake papers and spray with nonstick spray.

2. Make coffee to measure 1 cup. I use an espresso machine to make an Americano, which is watered down espresso, you could also use a tablespoon of instant espresso and boiling water to measure 1 cup.

3. Mix coffee and cocoa powder together. Set aside and allow to cool to room temp. Once it has cooled to room temp mix in sour cream and vanilla.

4. Using a standing mixer with paddle attachment, beat the butter on medium-high speed until smooth and shiny, about 30 seconds.

5. Gradually sprinkle in the sugar; beat until the mixture is fluffy and almost white, 3 to 5 minutes.

6. Add eggs one at a time, beating one full minute after each egg.

7. In a separate bowl, whisk together flour, baking soda and salt.

8. With the mixer on the lowest speed, add about a third of the dry ingredients to the batter, followed immediately by about a third of the cocoa mixture; mix until all ingredients are almost incorporated. Repeat the process twice more.

9. When batter appears blended, stop mixer and scrape sides of bowl with rubber spatula. Return mixer to low speed and beat until batter looks satiny, about 30 seconds.

10. Use a large scooper and place one scoop of batter into liners.

11. Bake for 23-30 minutes until a toothpick inserted into the middle comes out clean or with a crumb or two.

Instructions for coconut pecan filling

1. Place the egg yolks, sugar, cream, salt, vanilla, and butter in a pot over medium low heat. Cook, whisking frequently until it bubbles and foams up, lightens in color and then cook, whisking constantly for 2 more minutes.

2. Remove from heat, let cool, and then stir in the toasted coconut and toasted pecans.

3. Top each cooled cupcake with a heaping scoop of filling.

✎ NOTE:

Make the coconut pecan filling ahead of time. Store in the refrigerator for up to a month, thaw at room temperature for an hour to re-soften and top your cupcakes.

Carrot Cake Cupcakes

"Best Carrot Cake Ever" claim so many customers at my farmstand that I have lost count. Worth a try if you love carrot cake!

Makes 24

- 3-7 carrots, a little over a pound, this depends 100% on the size of your carrots. Weigh them BEFORE you grate them
- 2 ½ cups flour
- ½ teaspoon salt
- 1 ¼ teaspoons baking powder
- 1 teaspoon baking soda
- 1 teaspoon cinnamon
- ¼ teaspoon freshly grated nutmeg
- 1/8 teaspoon ground cloves
- 4 large eggs
- 1 cup brown sugar
- 1 cup sugar
- 1 ½ cups canola or vegetable oil
- 1 teaspoon vanilla

Cream Cheese Buttercream Frosting

- 1 stick softened butter, ½ cup
- 1 package of softened cream cheese, 8 ounces
- 1 teaspoon vanilla
- 1 tablespoon yogurt
- 3 ½ -4 ½ cups powdered sugar
- 1 tablespoon cream (optional)

1. Heat oven to 350 degrees. Line a 24-capacity muffin tin with cupcake papers and spray with nonstick spray.

2. In a food processor fitted with the large shredding disk, shred the carrots. Place them in a large bowl. Reserve the food processor, no need to clean it.

3. Add the flour, baking powder, baking soda, spices and salt and mix in with the carrots.

4. Put the metal blade into the food processor and add the sugars, oil, eggs and vanilla. Process until completely emulsified.

5. Scrape into the large bowl with carrots and flour mixture and mix just until no streaks of flour remain.

6. Bake for 22-28 minutes or until a toothpick inserted in the middle, barely comes out clean. You want them to be nice and moist.

7. Set aside to cool.

8. Place the cream cheese, butter, yogurt and vanilla in the bowl of a stand mixer. Blend until smooth.

9. Add 2 cups powdered sugar and mix until combined. Keep adding powdered sugar, ½ cup at a time, until frosting stiffens and makes slight peaks. This is a dense, rich frosting.

10. For a light whipped frosting, add the cream and whip in the mixer until the frosting lightens in texture. It should only take a minute or 2.

11. Top each cooled cupcake with a heaping scoop of frosting.

✎ NOTE:

Modify by adding any of these variations, together or individually, with the flour. 1 cup of toasted walnuts, raisins, toasted shredded coconut, pistachios, chopped dried apricots, cranberries or the zest of one orange.

Brown Butter Bourbon Pecan Pie

Pecan pie was one of my grandma's special talents. I can't remember a time when she was with us for a holiday that she didn't make one. The addition of brown butter and bourbon is something I added many years after she was gone. I think she would have loved it!

Makes 1 10-inch pie

Double Pie Crust

- (you will only use half of the dough for this recipe, and you can save the other half wrapped in plastic wrap in your fridge or freezer for another pie!)
- 3 cups flour
- 1 tablespoon sugar
- 1 teaspoon salt
- ½ cup butter, cold and cut into pieces (1/4 pound)
- 1 cup shortening
- 10-16 tablespoons ice water

1. Combine flour, sugar, salt, butter and shortening in a bowl using 2 butter knives or a pastry blender until the butter and shortening are the size of small peas.

2. Add 10 tablespoons of ice water and mix in with a fork to form a ball. If it's too dry to form a ball, dribble in more ice water, 1 tablespoon at a time until it comes together.

3. Knead the ball 4-5 times, return to the bowl, cover and refrigerate for at least 30 minutes. The colder the dough is, the easier it is to work with.

4. Shape dough into a ball, cover with plastic wrap, and put in the refrigerator for at least 30 minutes (colder is better here). This can be done up to 2 days before use.

5. When ready, remove from the fridge, divide in 2, and roll each into a circle large enough to fit your pan with about an inch or inch and half hanging over the side. I use a very large pie pan (I use a 11 inch pan with straight sides, so it can hold a lot).

6. Grease the pan and put the bottom crust in, very gently, don't stretch the dough.

Filling

- ¾ cup pecans
- 1 stick (1/2 cup) butter
- ½ cup light corn syrup
- 1 cup brown sugar
- 1 cup sugar
- 1 teaspoon vanilla
- ½ teaspoon salt
- 4 eggs
- 2 tablespoons bourbon (optional)

✎ NOTE:

Chocolate lovers can sprinkle ¼ cups mini or small chocolate chips over the pecans after they are toasted for a chocolate bourbon pecan pie.

1. Preheat the oven to 375º degrees. Roll out pie dough and put onto a greased pie plate. Make a nice edge, I usually do a scalloped edge with 3 of my fingers, 2 on 1 hand and 1 on the other.

2. Sprinkle the pecans all over the bottom of the crust. Bake the crust and the pecans at for 20 minutes. Then remove from the oven and set aside. Keep the oven on.

3. Add the butter in a small saucepan and melt at low heat. Watch it, and remove from heat when butter is browned (not burned) and nutty smelling. Let cool.

4. Place the cooled butter, corn syrup, sugars, vanilla, salt, bourbon (if using) and eggs in a blender and blend until smooth and emulsified and the sugars look dissolved.

5. Gently pour the ingredients of the blender over the pecans, being careful not to move them around too much into the process.

6. Bake for 45 minutes or until set. Let cool, and then chill.

Custard & Custard Pie

An adoration of eggs typically dictates a similar love affair with custard. This is very true for me. I like my custard served warm over fresh berries. My husband prefers it cold and dolloped over vanilla ice cream, and everyone loves a custard pie.

Serves 6

Custard

- 2 cups half and half
- 1 cup whole milk
- 3 eggs
- 3 tablespoons cornstarch
- 2/3 cup sugar
- 1-2 teaspoons vanilla

1. Put milk and half & half in a large glass bowl and microwave for about 3-4 minutes until hot and steaming, but not boiling.
2. In a separate bowl, whisk eggs, cornstarch and sugar until combined well. I like to use a silicone whisk for this.
3. Whisk a cup of hot milk mixture into egg mixture to temper the eggs. Then pour egg mixture into the hot milk mixture, whisking constantly, until combined well.
4. Return to microwave and cook on high in 30-second increments, whisking each time, until it starts to thicken. This will take a few minutes.
5. Remove from the microwave and whisk in the vanilla. Store in the refrigerator, covered until ready to use.
6. Serve warm or cold or pour into a prebaked pie shell and bake at 350 degrees for 15 minutes to make a traditional custard pie.

NOTE:

Add berries or poached stone fruit like nectarines or peaches to the pie before baking. For a brulee topping, evenly sprinkle the top of the pie with 3 tablespoons of sugar, and then place under the broiler or use a blow torch to caramelize the sugar.

To make the pie:

Pie Crust

- 2 cups flour
- 2 teaspoons sugar
- 1 teaspoon salt
- ¼ cup butter, cold and cut into pieces (½ stick)
- ½ cup shortening
- 8-12 tablespoons ice water

1. Mix flour, sugar and salt in a bowl.
2. Add butter and shortening and mix in with a pastry blender or 2 butter knives until the butter and shortening pieces are about the size of small peas. NO SMALLER or the crust will be dry and tough.
3. Add 8 tablespoons of ice water and mix in with a fork. If the dough does not come together in a ball, mix in up to 2 more tablespoons of ice water.
4. Shape dough into a ball, cover with plastic wrap, and put in the refrigerator for at least 30 minutes (colder is better here). This can be done up to 2 days before use.

Assemble the pie:

1. Preheat the oven to 350 degrees.
2. Grease your pie pan.
3. Roll out half the dough (save the other half for another pie) by scattering some flour on a clean dry surface (I use my kitchen counter). Roll it out, flipping and rotating often, until you have a circle that is an inch and half larger than your pie pan.
4. Fold it in half and place it in your pan, unfolding it so it is centered. Ans then crimp the edge with your fingers so it looks pretty.
5. Top the crust with a piece of greased parchment and put another pie pan on top of as a weight (or use dried beans as a weight). Bake for 20 minutes.
6. Take the crust out of the oven, remove the weights and the parchment. Pour in the custard to the edge of the crimped part, and put back in the oven for 30 minutes. Let cool, and then refrigerate. Serve cold.

Green Tea Ice Cream

Whether you enjoy green tea with your sushi, matcha green tea lattes or smoothies or just love the idea of green ice cream, you simply cannot go through life without tasting this delectable treat. It's a wonderfully delicious end to any meal!

Serves 4

- 2 cups whole milk
- 1 ¼ cups cream
- 2 tablespoons matcha green tea powder
- 5 eggs yolks
- ¾ cup sugar
- 1 ½ tablespoons cornstarch
- 1 teaspoon vanilla

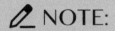 NOTE:

Store matcha green tea powder in the freezer or refrigerator so it doesn't lose its vibrant green color and flavor.

1. Combine milk, cream, and green tea in a microwave safe bowl and heat in the microwave for 3-4 minutes until hot and steaming.
2. Whisk until smooth and let steep on the counter for 30 minutes.
3. Whisk egg yolks with sugar and cornstarch in a separate bowl, until thick and pale.
4. Temper with the hot milk / cream mixture by slowly whisking in about ¾ cup at a time. Then add the egg mixture BACK into the milk / cream mixture, whisking as you go.
5. Return to the microwave and cook in 30-60 second increments, whisking each time until it thickens (about 160 degrees). Do not boil.
6. Whisk in the vanilla., cover with plastic and refrigerate 8 hours or overnight.
7. Process in ice cream maker about 40-60 minutes and then freeze until hard.

Salted Caramel

As ice cream toppings go, caramel has always been a love of mine, but when it becomes salted caramel, it goes right to the top of my list. Salted Caramel might just be a perfect food and it is simply the best way to have vanilla ice cream, period. What do I say about this recipe, except it is ALWAYS in my fridge.

Makes 2 pints

- 1 ½ cups sugar
- ½ cup water
- 1 ¼ cups heavy cream
- 1 teaspoon salt (use fleur de sel, if you can get it)
- 1 teaspoon vanilla

1. Add the sugar and water to a large saucepan. This recipe will expand exponentially, you'll need the room.

2. Heat at medium heat, do NOT stir. Swirl the pan a bit so the sugar dissolves and watch it closely over the 15-30 minutes it takes for the sugar water to turn to syrup and then darken to caramel. Watch it closely. It turns from yellow to amber quickly and it can go to blackened in an instant, which will ruin it and you'll have to start over.

3. Meanwhile, add your salt to the cream in a measuring cup and warm it in the microwave. Stir gently to dissolve the salt and then add the vanilla. Set aside.

4. Once the sugar-water mixture turns caramel colored, remove it from the heat. It will smell amazing and be SUPER HOT.

5. With the caramel off the heat, pour in the cream mixture and immediately STAND BACK as it bubbles and expands.

6. Count to 20 before you approach the pot again, it may keep spewing burning steam and expanding a few seconds longer than you expect.

7. When it calms down, put the pot back on the burner, turn it on low, and stir gently with a silicone whisk until smooth and slightly simmering. Turn off the heat.

8. Let it cool enough so you can taste it. Taste it and adjust with salt and vanilla to your preference.

9. Pour into a pint-sized jar and let it cool to room temperature. Then cover, label, and put in the refrigerator.

✎ NOTE:

Salted Caramel MUST be kept in the refrigerator and will be good for many months. Reheat in the microwave.

Salted Chocolate Chip Cookies (gluten-free, vegan)

Yep! These are salted chocolate chip cookies that are soy free, nut free, wheat free and vegan. HOW can they possibly taste good? Well, part of the answer is I don't really know, but the finished product surprised the heck out of me and many friends and family with its deliciousness. The addition of potato chips adds an appealing crispiness and saltiness that has me wanting more.

"Even My husband loves these cookies and he never eats the gluten free stuff I make. My new favorite cookie is salted chocolate chip cookies. They were very easy to make." Katie Tsao

Makes 24

- 2 cups loosely packed or sifted oat flour (make sure it is very loosely packed or your cookies will end up dry)
- ½ teaspoon baking soda
- ¼ teaspoon kosher salt
- 1 tablespoon flaxseed meal (ground flaxseeds)
- ¼ cup vanilla coconut milk
- 1/3 cup canola oil
- ½ cup brown sugar
- ¼ cup sugar
- 1 teaspoon vanilla
- ¾ cup mini dairy, nut, soy and egg free chocolate chips
- 1 cup kettle potato chips, crushed (about 1/3 cup crushed)

1. Preheat oven to 375 degrees.
2. In a medium bowl, mix oat flour, baking soda and salt.
3. In a separate bowl, whisk flaxseed meal and vanilla coconut milk.
4. Whisk in canola oil, sugars and vanilla until emulsified (the oil doesn't separate and it is a little opaque). This should only take about 20 seconds if you are using a silicone whisk.
5. Combine wet and dry ingredients, and then gently mix in chocolate chips and potato chips.
6. Drop batter by tablespoons onto ungreased (parchment lined, for less mess) cookie sheets and bake for 10-15 minutes, until golden.
7. Cool for 5 minutes and then remove to a rack to cool the rest of the way.

NOTE:

The batter for these cookies should not be dry and crumbly at all. If it is, it will make dry cookies. If you notice this, before you form and bake the cookies, add more oil, 1 teaspoon at a time, until the dough is no longer crumbly.

Peanut Butter Toffee

Here's the thing about this toffee, it is crisp and light while being rich and dense. It has chocolate on top, making it feel like one of those lovely candy bark things you can't get enough of around the holidays. It has a peanut butter filling that is strongly reminiscent of a popular peanut butter and chocolate cup-shaped candy. It is, dare I say it, obsession-worthy!

Makes about 40

- 45-50 saltine crackers
- 3 sticks, ¾ pound butter
- 1 ½ cups brown sugar
- 12 ounces chocolate chips, semi-sweet, bittersweet, dark or milk. Do not use white chocolate, it doesn't melt correctly for this recipe.
- ¼ cup sliced almonds – optional

Peanut Butter Filling

- 1 cup creamy peanut butter
- 2 sticks butter, melted
- 1 ½ cups graham cracker crumbs
- ¾ pound powdered sugar

1. Preheat the oven to 350 degrees. Line a cookie sheet | jelly roll pan with foil and grease it.
2. Arrange 40-50 saltine crackers in one layer on the bottom of the pan.
3. Melt 3 sticks of unsalted butter in a saucepan. Add 1 ½ cups of brown sugar and then boil, string constantly for exactly 3 minutes.
4. Quickly pour butter-sugar mixture over the crackers and spread in an even layer.
5. Immediately put it in the oven and bake for 12 minutes. Remove from the oven and cool completely.
6. Mix 1 cup creamy peanut butter, 2 sticks melted butter, 1 ½ cups graham cracker crumbs and ¾ powdered sugar in a bowl. Set aside.
7. When the toffee is cool, very carefully spread the filling layer on top of the toffee layer.
8. Sprinkle 12 ounces chocolate chips on top and put back into a warm oven for about a minute or 2 or until they look glossy.
9. Remove from the oven as soon as chips start to melt or else the peanut butter filling will melt too.
10. Fully spread chocolate over the top of the toffee. Sprinkle with nuts of your choice. Let cool. Cut into squares or break into bark.
11. Store in an airtight container in the refrigerator or freezer to extend the freshness a bit.

✎ NOTE:

Optional toppings include nuts, seeds, crushed heath bars, coconut, sprinkles, candy canes or even candied bacon.

Flourless Chocolate Cake (gluten free)

The first time I had anything like this, I was at a birthday party in Florence, Italy. The chocolate flavor in this cake is what blew me away. I couldn't wait to create a version to make back at home. My favorite dark chocolate to use for this recipe is Callebaut dark chocolate, and the best way to serve is with a big pile of fresh raspberries on top. It's gorgeous, fancy and delicious.

Serves 12

- 8 ounces dark chocolate, chopped coarsely, or in chips
- 10 tablespoons butter
- 2/3 cup sugar
- 1/3 cup cold water
- 1/3 cup sugar
- 3 large eggs

NOTE:

Use a gluten-free chocolate to keep the cake truly GF!

1. Preheat the oven to 250 degrees. Grease an 8-inch springform pan with removable sides, line with a parchment paper circle, and grease again.

2. Place the dark chocolate, butter, 2/3 cup sugar and 1/3 cup water in a microwave safe bowl, and heat in 30 second increments, stirring each time until it is melted and smooth. Set aside to cool slightly.

3. Place the eggs and 1/3 cup sugar in a mixing bowl and beat for about 6 minutes with the whisk attachment until the mixture has quadrupled in volume and is thick and a pale, yellow color.

4. Turn the mixer on low, and then add the chocolate mixture slowly. Continue beating until the ingredients are just incorporated.

5. Pour the mixture into the prepared pan.

6. Place the pan on a cookie sheet with a rim, lined with a kitchen towel. Place in the oven, and then pour hot water into the cookie sheet to make a water bath for the cake to cook in. You want the water to come up 1/2 to 1 inch up the outside of the springform pan.

7. Bake for 65 minutes. The cake is ready when you touch the top and the batter doesn't stick to your finger, and it looks sort of dry and shiny.

8. Remove from the oven and leave the cake pan in the water bath and allow to cool on kitchen counter until completely cold.

9. Remove cake pan from water bath. Dry the pan. Slide a knife around the inside of the pan and remove the sides.

10. Place a plate, larger than the cake, over the cake and flip the plate.

11. The top of the cake now becomes the bottom. Refrigerate 3 hours or overnight. Dust with powdered sugar just before serving.

Pots de Crème (gluten free)

This is a super impressive and incredibly delicious chocolate dessert. The dessert itself seems like it should be complicated and yet it could not be simpler to make. It tastes very refined with the German chocolate and looks beautiful served in pretty little ceramic or glass cups.

Serves 4-6

- 1 bar (4 ounces) German chocolate
- 1 teaspoon sugar
- ½ cup heavy cream
- 2 egg yolks, slightly beaten
- 1 teaspoon cognac, bourbon or Grand Marnier (optional)
- ½ teaspoon vanilla
- whipped cream for topping

1. Mix chocolate, sugar and cream in a non-metallic bowl. Microwave in 30-second increments, stirring after each one, until mixture becomes smooth and blended.

2. Pour hot mixture slowly into egg yolks, stirring constantly. Blend in vanilla.

3. Pour into demitasse cups and refrigerate until chilled, about an hour.

✎ NOTE:

Another fun option for the liquor is Chambord, which is raspberry, or Kahlua, which has a coffee flavor.

Spiced Pear Custard Brulé Pie

There's this poached pear recipe that my parents made for their very fancy dinner parties. They would peel whole pears with the stem intact, poach the pears in a spiced liquid and wine, and then serve them with a creamy velvety sauce. This delectable pie is my replication of that flavor and fanciness!

Serves 6

- 1 pie dough recipe
- 2 pounds pears, washed, cored, and sliced thin
- 1 cup sugar
- 1 teaspoon cinnamon
- a pinch of ground star anise
- a pinch of ground nutmeg
- a pinch of ground allspice
- a pinch of ground ginger
- a pinch of ground cloves
- 2 tablespoons tapioca
- 1 teaspoon lemon zest
- 1 tablespoon lemon juice, freshly squeezed

Custard Topping

- 1 ½ cups half and half
- 1/3 cup sugar
- 1 ½ tablespoons cornstarch
- 1 teaspoon vanilla
- 1 whole egg + 1 yolk

Brulé Topping

- 2 tablespoons sugar
- a blowtorch or your broiler

Make the filling

1. Add the pears, sugar, cinnamon, ground spices, tapioca, lemon zest and lemon juice together in a large bowl.

2. Set aside to marinate while you make the custard and build the pie.

Make the custard

1. Put the half and half in a medium saucepan over low heat and warm, stirring periodically until it starts to steam.

2. Meanwhile, in a separate bowl, blend the sugar cornstarch vanilla egg and egg yolk with a whisk.

3. Once the half and half is steaming, take a ladle of it and drizzle it into the egg and sugar mixture, whisking constantly until completely combined.

4. Take another ladle and do the same until the egg mix is slightly warmer than room temperature. Then, drizzle the egg mixture slowly, back into the half and half while whisking constantly. This is called tempering the eggs and it keeps them from cooking and scrambling in your custard.

5. Take another ladle and do the same until the egg mix is slightly warmer than room temperature. Then, drizzle the egg mixture slowly, back into the half and half while whisking constantly. This is called tempering the eggs and it keeps them from cooking and scrambling in your custard.

6. Once all the egg mix has been blended into the half and half, stir constantly until the custard thickens and has the consistency of yogurt or a little thinner.

7. Remove from the heat, and place in the refrigerator in a bowl with plastic wrap covering it. Make sure the plastic wrap is directly touching the custard so that it does not form a skin.

Make the crust & build the pie

1. Mix flour, sugar and salt in a bowl.
2. Add butter and shortening and mix in with a pastry blender or 2 butter knives until the butter and shortening pieces are about the size of small peas. NO SMALLER or the crust will be dry and tough.
3. Add 5 tablespoons of ice water and mix in with a fork. If the dough does not come together in a ball, mix in up to 2 more tablespoons of ice water.
4. Shape dough into a ball, cover with plastic wrap, and put in the refrigerator for at least 30 minutes (colder is better here). This can be done up to 2 days before use.
5. Preheat the oven to 375 degrees.
6. Roll out the bottom crust and place it in a greased 9-10 inch pie pan.
7. Add the pear mixture. It won't be full, and it should not heap over the level of the edge of the pie crust.
8. Bake for 30 minutes, on a baking sheet to catch the drips.
9. Remove from the oven and lower the oven temperature to 350 degrees.
10. Add the custard over the top to completely fill the crust. It's okay if you don't use it all.
11. Return the pie to the oven for another 25 minutes. When it is done, the custard will look slightly cracked. Remove from the oven and let cool.
12. Once the pie has cooled, sprinkle the custard portion with two tablespoons of sugar.
13. Using a broiler or a blowtorch, caramelize the sugar to make the brulee.
14. If you are using the blowtorch, slowly start melting the sugar, not staying in one place for too long until all of the sugar has hardened and looks a little bit liquid and golden in color. Take your time.
15. If using the broiler, place the pie with the sugar on top rack, under the broiler and keep a very close eye on it. You might have to keep rotating it to make sure that the edges don't burn while you are melting the sugar.
16. Serve immediately or put the pie in the refrigerator and serve within four hours so the topping stays hard. If you keep it in the refrigerator for too long, the brulee topping might turn liquid again.

✎ NOTE:

To make this pie a straight Spiced Pear Pie, without the custard and brulee topping, use the filling measurements below and add a top pie crust. Cut for venting and sprinkle with a bit of sugar. Bake at 375 degrees for one hour or until golden and bubbling. Modify filling ingredients as follows:

- 3 pounds pears, washed, cored, and sliced thin
- 1 ¼ cups sugar
- 1 teaspoon cinnamon
- 1/8 teaspoon ground star anise
- 1/8 teaspoon ground nutmeg
- ¼ teaspoon ground allspice
- ¼ teaspoon ground ginger
- 1/8 teaspoon ground cloves
- 3 tablespoons tapioca
- zest and juice of 1 lemon

Cheesecake

We make and sell a lot of cheesecakes at my farmstand. One of my favorite things to do with leftover cheesecake (plain, lemon, fruit, chocolate, or other flavor) is chunk it up and smush it into vanilla ice cream. Then I have cheesecake ice cream, VOILA! It's so delicious!

Serves 12

- 2 cups graham cracker crumbs
- ¼ cup powdered sugar
- 1 stick butter, melted
- 1/8 teaspoon kosher salt
- 1/8 teaspoon cinnamon
- 6 packages cream cheese, 8 ounces each at room temperature
- 2 cups powdered sugar
- 5 large eggs, at room temperature
- 1 tablespoon vanilla
- 1 ¼ cups sour cream, at room temperature

1. Preheat the oven to 325 degrees and adjust the rack to the middle of the oven.
2. Melt the butter in a medium microwave-safe bowl.
3. Add the graham crackers, powdered sugar, kosher salt, cinnamon and combine to make the crust.
4. Pour the crust mixture into a 10" x 4" round springform pan and press into the bottom and halfway up the sides using your fingers.
5. In a large mixer using the paddle attachment, beat the room temperature cream cheese and powdered sugar until creamy.
6. Add in the room temperature eggs one at a time and beat until incorporated after each egg.
7. Add the vanilla and the room temperature sour cream and beat until just Incorporated.
8. Pour the cheesecake mixture into the crust and even off the top.
9. Place the springform pan on a sheet pan large enough to hold it.
10. Bake for 50 minutes until the top is no longer be glossy and the center is jiggly.
11. Turn off the oven and crack the oven door. Let the cheesecake sit in the oven for 45 minutes.
12. Remove the cheesecake from the oven and run a sharp knife between the cheesecake and the pan, to ensure the cheesecake doesn't stick.
13. Leave on the counter for one hour.
14. Cover loosely with plastic wrap and refrigerate for at least eight hours.
15. THEN, remove the springform pan sides, slice and serve.

French Silk Pie

Standing the test of time, French silk pie is a rich, dense, melt-in-your-mouth chocolate, reminiscent of a firm chocolate mousse in a delicate yet chewy pecan meringue crust. It's super fancy and my brother's number one choice for dessert every single year on his birthday.

Serves 6

- 4 egg whites, room temperature
- ¼ teaspoon cream of tartar
- 1 cup sugar
- ½ cup chopped pecans
- ¼ pound butter, softened
- 2 eggs
- ½ cup sugar
- ¼ teaspoon vanilla
- 2 squares (2 ounces) unsweetened chocolate, melted

1. Preheat the oven to 275 degrees.
2. Beat room temperature egg whites until stiff but not dry.
3. Add sugar slowly, beating until stiff enough to hold a peak.
4. Add cream of tartar and fold in pecans.
5. Spread into a greased 10-inch pie pan.
6. Bake for 1 hour at 275 degrees. Turn off the oven and let cool in the oven for one hour. Remove and set aside to cool the rest of the way.
7. Cream butter. Add sugar, ¼ cup at a time.
8. Beat in chocolate.
9. Add eggs, one at a time and beat 5 minutes (YES FIVE WHOLE MINUTES) after each egg, then add the vanilla.
10. Pour in cooled crust. Top with ½ pint of heavy cream, whipped.
11. Garnish with pecans and grated chocolate.

Lemon Bars

These should not be so delicious for how simple and basic they are to make. They are delicate yet firm, chewy and crisp, tart and mild, and what you always wanted in a lemon bar.

Makes 32

- 2 cups flour
- 1 cup butter
- 2 cups powdered sugar
- 2 cups sugar
- 4 beaten eggs
- 1 tablespoon flour
- 1 teaspoon baking powder
- zest and juice of two lemons

1. Preheat the oven to 350 degrees.
2. Mix flour, butter and powdered sugar.
3. Firmly pack in a 9 by 13 pan and bake for 15-20 minutes.
4. Meanwhile, mix the sugar, eggs, flour, baking powder, lemon zest and lemon juice together.
5. Remove the crust from the oven and immediately pour the wet mixture over the hot crust.
6. Bake for 22-35 minutes, remove from oven and let cool before cutting.

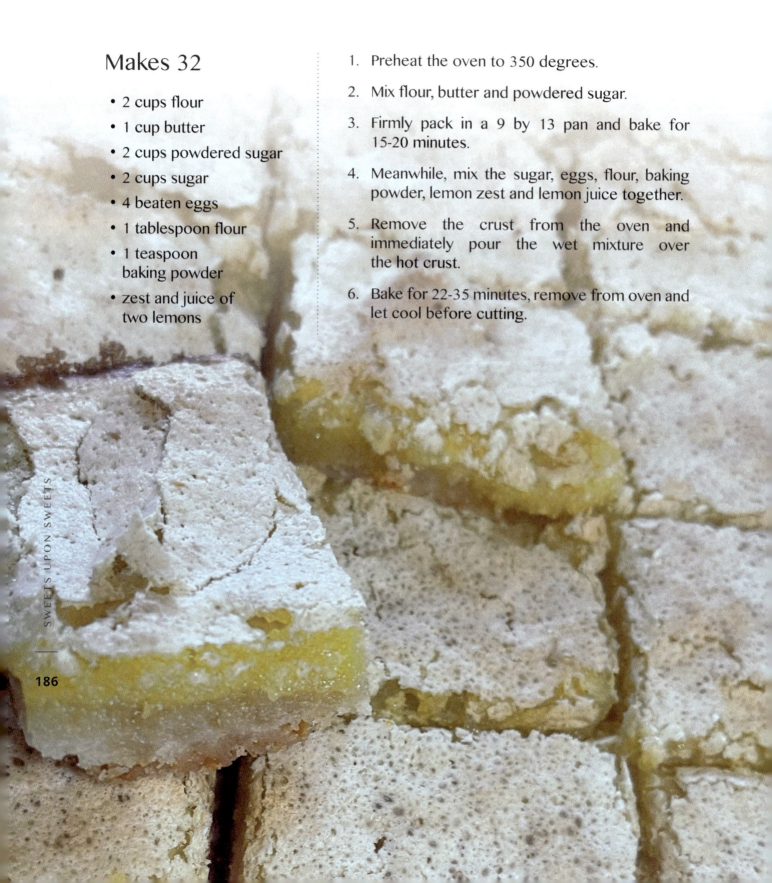

Keto Lemon Bars

When we first opened the farmstand, we sold fresh produce, eggs, plants and baked goods. As my clientele grew, I started getting requests to make new items. Insert these lemon bars, along with my pumpkin bars. These are the very first keto items we offered at the farmstand and I couldn't be prouder! A super popular item, they have an assertive lemon flavor and a creamy texture, with a biscuit-like crust.

Makes 32

- 4 cups almond flour
- ½ cup monkfruit powdered sweetener
- 1 cup melted butter, 2 sticks
- 9 large eggs
- 1 cup sour cream
- 4 medium or 3 large lemons, zested and juiced, to make 1 cups lemon juice and about a heaping tablespoon of lemon zest
- 1 tablespoon vanilla
- 1 cup almond flour
- 1 cup monkfruit powdered sweetener

1. Preheat oven to 325 degrees and line a 9x13 pan with parchment paper and cooking spray.
2. In a medium bowl, put the melted butter. Add the almond flour and ½ cup monk fruit sweetener, blend until combined.
3. Press mixture into prepared pan in an even layer.
4. In a blender, combine eggs, sour cream, lemon juice, zest and vanilla.
5. Add the almond flour and 1 cup monk fruit sweetener, blend until smooth.
6. Pour filling over crust and bake until filling is set, 30-40 mins.
7. Let cool to room temperature, then refrigerate until set, about 2 hours. Dust with powdered monk fruit sweetener, (if desired).
8. Slice into bars and serve.

Lemon Lemon Cupcakes

Tart, moist and fresh lemony lemon all at once! This lemon cake is enhanced by the addition of lemon simple syrup that gets drizzled on the cake after it is baked for an extra lemon punch. The whipped cream cheese buttercream frosting adds a creamy sweet tang. I love lemon desserts, and this cake checks all of my lemon boxes!

Makes 24

- 8 ounces buttermilk at room temperature
- 3 ounces vegetable oil, 85 g
- 3 large eggs, room temperature
- zest and juice of 2 large lemons, ½ cup juice
- ½ teaspoon lemon extract
- 13 ounces all-purpose flour
- 11 ounces granulated sugar
- ½ teaspoon salt
- 2 teaspoons baking powder
- ½ teaspoon baking soda
- 8 ounces softened butter, 2 sticks

Cream Cheese Buttercream Frosting

- 1 stick butter softened, ½ cup
- 1 package of cream cheese softened, 8 ounces
- 1 teaspoon vanilla
- 1 tablespoon yogurt
- 3 ½ -4 ½ cups powdered sugar
- 1 tablespoon cream (optional)

Lemon Syrup

- 1 cup of granulated sugar
- ½ cup freshly squeezed lemon juice
- ½ cup water

1. Preheat oven to 350 degrees. Line a 24-capacity muffin tin with cupcake papers and spray with nonstick spray.
2. Divide the buttermilk into two measuring cups. Each should be at least a 2-cups measuring cup because you are going to add more ingredients to each.
3. To one of the buttermilks, add the oil.
4. To the other buttermilk, add the lemon zest and juice, the eggs and the lemon extract. Set aside.
5. In a mixer with the paddle attachment on low, add the flour, sugar, salt, baking powder and baking soda.
6. Add the butter in about 8 chunks, continue mixing until it looks crumbly.
7. Add the buttermilk-oil mixture and mix for 5 full minutes.
8. Pause and scrape down the bowl a couple of times during the mixing process to make sure the batter gets smooth before the next step.
9. Add the buttermilk, egg, lemon mixture in a slow stream and mix until thoroughly combined. It might look a little curdled, and that's ok.
10. Pour the batter into the cupcake pan. I use a scoop to get them even. Bake for 20-25 minutes or until a toothpick comes out clean.
11. Remove from the oven and allow to cool for 10 minutes.
12. While cakes are cooling, make the lemon syrup. Combine sugar, lemon juice and water in a small microwave safe measuring cup.
13. Cook in the microwave for 30 second intervals, taking out and stirring with each interval, until sugar is dissolved.
14. Poke each cupcake with a fork or a toothpick, and spoon 1 teaspoon lemon syrup over each one.

FOR THE FROSTING:

15. Place the cream cheese, butter, yogurt and vanilla in the bowl of a stand mixer. Blend until smooth.
16. Add 2 cups powdered sugar and mix until combined. Keep adding powdered sugar, ½ cup at a time, until frosting stiffens and makes slight peaks. This is a dense, rich frosting.
17. For the light whipped frosting which is characteristic for these cupcakes, add the cream and whip in the mixer until the frosting lightens in texture. It should only take a minute or 2.
18. Once the cakes are cooled, frost with cream cheese buttercream and top each cupcake with a small section of a slice of lemon.

✎ NOTE:

Use 2 8-inch or 2 9-inch pans to make cakes. Bake for 30 minutes.

Keto Pumpkin Bars

I love a good fall spice cake, especially with a frosting. These pumpkin bars have the perfect flavor and moist cake texture, and are surprisingly gluten free, sugar free and very low in carbs. They are popular at my farmstand all year round!

Makes 64

- 5 eggs, beaten
- 1 cup extra virgin olive oil
- 1 cup granulated monk fruit sweetener
- 1 ½ cups Libby's canned pumpkin puree
- 2 cups almond flour
- 1 teaspoon baking soda
- 1 teaspoon baking powder
- ½ teaspoon kosher salt
- 1 teaspoon pie spice or a cinnamon blend spice of your choice that includes cloves and ginger.
- 16 ounces cream cheese, softened
- 1 stick room temperature butter, 8 tablespoons
- 1 cup powdered monkfruit sweetener
- 1 teaspoon vanilla extract
- ¼ teaspoon maple extract
- 2 tablespoons heavy cream

1. Preheat the oven to 350 degrees and grease a regular size (around 18x12) sheet pan. The sheet size can be a little flexible if you monitor baking time.

2. In a mixer with the paddle attachment add eggs, olive oil, granulated monk fruit sweetener and pumpkin puree. Beat until well combined.

3. Add almond flour, baking soda, baking powder, salt and pumpkin pie spice. Combine well.

4. Pour evenly on a baking sheet and bake for 25-30 minutes.

5. Meanwhile, combine the cream cheese, butter, powdered monkfruit, vanilla and maple extract in a medium bowl and beat with a mixer with a whisk attachment.

6. Add heavy cream and whip for 3-4 minutes until light.

7. Frost the WARM cake. Put small globs all over the cake and spread with a frosting spreader or butter knife. A spatula does not work very well.

8. Cool completely, then cut and keep refrigerated.

✎ NOTE:

Cut these into 64 little bars, each one is just 1 carb!

Keto Cheesecake

This recipe would not be in here were it not for my dear friend Allison. She is borderline obsessed with this delicious cheesecake and likes to serve it to friends and family and at large events when she knows there will be guests who are on keto diets, who are gluten free, or who are diabetic. It's such a treat to have a sweet creamy cheesecake, it feels like cheating but it's not!

Serves 10-12

- 2 cups almond flour
- ¼ cup powdered monkfruit sweetener
- 1 stick butter, melted
- 1/8 teaspoon kosher salt
- 6 packages room temperature cream cheese, 8 ounces each
- 2 cups powdered monkfruit sweetener
- 5 large room temperature eggs
- 1 tablespoon vanilla
- 1 ¼ cups room temperature sour cream

 NOTE:

For lemon cheesecake, add the zest and juice of one lemon to the filling with the eggs.

1. Preheat the oven to 325 degrees, adjust the rack to the middle of the oven.
2. Melt the butter in a medium microwave-safe bowl. Add almond flour, ¼ cup monkfruit, salt and combine.
3. Pour the mixture into a greased 10" x 4" round springform pan and press in the bottom and halfway up the sides using your fingers.
4. In a large mixer using the paddle attachment, beat the room temperature cream cheese and 2 cups powdered monk fruit sweetener until creamy.
5. Add in the room temperature eggs one at a time and beat until incorporated and completely smooth after each egg.
6. Add in the vanilla and the room temperature sour cream and beat until just Incorporated.
7. Pour the cheesecake mixture into the crust and even off the top.
8. Place the springform pan on a sheet pan large enough to hold it.
9. Bake for 50 minutes until the top is no longer glossy and the center is jiggly. Turn off the oven and crack the oven door. Let the cheesecake sit in the oven for 45 minutes.
10. Remove the cheesecake from the oven and run a sharp knife between the cheesecake and the pan, to ensure the cheesecake doesn't stick.
11. Leave on the counter for one hour.
12. Cover loosely with plastic wrap and refrigerate for at least eight hours.
13. THEN, remove the springform pan sides, slice and serve.

Chocolate Whiskey Cupcakes with Salted Whiskey Caramel Frosting - Gluten Free

When I introduced alcohol infused cupcakes at the farmstand, they were only available gluten free. I wanted to give my gluten free customers a treat that felt exclusive. I never realized that my gluten eaters would love them too, discovering that it was ok to enjoy a gluten free cake even if you weren't gluten free. All of my friends and family that have tried these have loved them and had no idea that these cupcakes were gluten free.

- ½ cups regular olive oil, nothing too strong
- 3 ounces of dark chocolate, in chips or chopped
- 1/3 cup of cocoa powder
- ¾ cup of King Arthur gluten-free flour (3 1/2 ounces)
- ¾ teaspoon baking powder
- ½ teaspoon baking soda
- ½ teaspoon xanthan gum
- ½ teaspoon kosher salt
- 2 large eggs
- 2 teaspoons vanilla extract
- ¾ cup of sugar
- ¼ cup milk
- ¼ cup bourbon whiskey

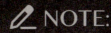 NOTE:

if you have a gluten allergy, check with your doctor before consuming bourbon whiskey

Salted Whiskey Caramel

- 1 cup granulated sugar
- 2 tablespoons water
- 1 tablespoon corn syrup
- 6 tablespoons butter
- ½ cup heavy cream
- 1 teaspoon kosher salt
- 3 tablespoons bourbon whiskey

- Frosting
- 2 tablespoons caramel (above)
- 2 sticks room temperature butter, 16 tablespoons
- 2 ½ cups of powdered sugar
- 1 teaspoon vanilla
- 1 tablespoon heavy cream

---

1. Preheat the oven to 350 degrees. Line a 24-capacity muffin tin with cupcake papers and spray with nonstick spray.
2. Microwave oil, chocolate, and cocoa together in a bowl at 50% power, stirring occasionally until melted, about 2 minutes.
3. Whisk mixture until smooth, then set aside to cool slightly.
4. In a separate bowl, mix gluten-free flour, baking powder, baking soda, xanthan gum, and salt together.
5. In a large bowl, whisk eggs and vanilla together.
6. Whisk in the sugar until combined.
7. Mix cooled chocolate mixture with milk and whiskey until combined.
8. Add in the flour blend mixture until the batter is thoroughly combined and smooth.
9. Let the batter sit for 30 minutes. This step allows the gluten-free flour to absorb the liquid ingredients in the batter and it makes it much more moist and not grainy.
10. Using an ice cream scoop or a large spoon, portion the batter evenly into the prepared muffin tin.
11. Bake until a toothpick inserted into the center of the cupcakes comes out clean, 16 to 20 minutes, rotating them halfway through baking.
12. Let cupcakes cool in the muffin tin for about 10 minutes and then remove and let cool completely, about an hour before frosting them.
13. Meanwhile, place the sugar, water and corn syrup in a large saucepan. This recipe will expand exponentially, you'll need the room.

14. Heat at medium to medium-high heat, do NOT stir. Swirl the pan a bit so the sugar dissolves and watch it closely over the 15-30 minutes it takes for the sugar water to turn to syrup and then darken to caramel. Watch it closely. It turns from yellow to amber quickly and it can go to blackened in an instant, which will ruin it and you'll have to start over.

15. Meanwhile, add your cream, butter, salt in a measuring cup and warm it in the microwave. Stir gently to dissolve the salt and then add the bourbon. Set aside.

16. Once the sugar, water and corn syrup mixture turns caramel colored, remove it from the heat and pour in the cream and butter mixture and immediately STAND BACK as it bubbles and expands.

17. Wait a full minute before you approach the pot again, it may keep spewing burning steam and expanding a few seconds longer than you expect.

18. When it calms down, put the pot back on the burner on medium heat, and stir gently to combine. Once it is smooth, remove from heat and cool completely.

19. For the frosting, place the butter, powdered sugar, caramel, and vanilla in a medium mixing bowl. Beat using the whisk attachment until smooth and combined.

20. Add the cream and beat for 4 minutes until light and fluffy.

21. Frost the cupcakes and then drizzle with the caramel. Reserve extra caramel and any extra frosting for a future use.

 **NOTE:**

Use Ritual bourbon for an alcohol-free cupcake!

Chapter Seven

Adrienne's Afterthoughts

It's not that these recipes don't belong anywhere else, it's that they are each so special in their own right. The best fragrant and chewy Italian bread (Focaccia), the Bread and Butter pickles that evoke summer memories with Grandma, the appetizer that always steals the show (Habanero Apricot Jelly with cheese and crackers), and of course the Super Elderberry Syrup that you want to have on hand BEFORE you get a cold this season. Finally, we absolutely cannot close this collection without the creamy, spicy flavor and heady aroma of the ultimate White Chicken Chili.

"Always go with your passions. Never ask yourself if it's realistic or not."

- DEEPAK CHOPRA

Adrienne's Afterthoughts

1. Focaccia 200
2. Bone Broth 202
3. Fig Pecan Jam with Port 203
4. Homemade Vanilla 204
5. Apricot Mustard 207
6. Farmstand Guacamole 209
7. Spicy Pickled Green Beans 210
8. Bread & Butter Pickles 211
9. Balsamic Onions 212
10. Tuna Fish with Pickled Red Onions & Pepitas 213
11. Fresh Garlic Dill Pickles 214
12. Habanero Apricot Jelly 215
13. Pineapple Jalapeno Jelly 216
14. Super Elderberry Syrup 217
15. Peach Bourbon Barbecue Sauce 218
16. Moroccan Chickpea Stew 220
17. White Chicken Chili 223

Focaccia

After having spent so many years in Italy, I felt my farmstand needed a nice Italian bread. Full disclosure, I picked focaccia because it was the least cumbersome of all the recipes I researched and the easiest to customize. Sometimes, the simplest is the way to go, because I never turned back. This bread is chewy and flavorful, the smell wafting from the oven while baking is intoxicating, and the crispness from the olive oil crust is musical and luscious.

Makes 2 loaves

Sponge

- ½ cups organic flour
- 1/3 water, at room temperature
- ¼ teaspoon active dry yeast. I use Red Star yeast.

Bread

- 2 ½ cups organic flour, plus more later for shaping / forming to loaves
- 1 1/3 cups room temperature water
- 1 teaspoon yeast
- 4 teaspoons kosher salt. I use Diamond Crystal or Morton's kosher salt.
- 4 tablespoons extra virgin olive oil
- 1 ½ teaspoons kosher salt, for later

1. In a medium glass mixing bowl. Mix the ingredients for the sponge with a fork until blended.

2. Cover the bowl with plastic wrap and leave at room temperature; on the kitchen counter is good, for 6-18 hours. This step is super flexible, making it work for your schedule. The yeast should bubble up and then the goopy contents should collapse a little.

3. Next, add the remaining flour, water and yeast and mix again with a fork until blended. Let sit for 20 minutes.

4. Sprinkle with 2 teaspoons of salt and mix again. Let sit for another 20 minutes.

5. Then, using a silicone spatula sprayed with cooking spray (or if you are lucky enough to have one, a Danish dough whisk), flop the dough around 4 or 5 times to mix and knead it. Wait 45 minutes and do it again.

6. Heat the oven to 500 degrees. Make sure it reaches temperature before you bake the bread. It should be 45 minutes for it to really get to the right temperature, even if it says it's ready before that, let it heat for a good 45 minutes.

7. Put 2 tablespoons of olive oil in each of 2 9-10 inch pie tins or pie plates. Sprinkle each with ¾ teaspoon salt. Set aside.

8. Put a lot of flour on your countertop or on a silicone mat or a piece of parchment paper.

9. Dump the dough onto the flour. Use your fingers to toss it lightly so the whole thing has a thin coat of flour on the outside. It will be a goopy mess.

10. Using a bench scraper or a butter knife, cut the dough in half. Put half in each pie pan, and then flip it over so that the oil and salt cover the outside of the dough.

11. Poke each one with a fork about 20 times. Let it puff up again in the pan for about 10 minutes and then bake for 20 minutes or until golden.

✐ NOTE:

Use organic flour, the flavor profile is noticeably different otherwise. Topping options are limitless, my favorites are 2 tablespoons chopped rosemary and some kalamata olives, roasted garlic cloves, parmesan and chopped parsley, sun dried tomatoes and oregano, pepitas, or just a sprinkling of ©Everything Bagel seasoning (which is typically a combination of poppy seeds, sesame seeds, dried garlic and dried onion).

Bone Broth

I will not even attempt to share all the wisdom that has been dropped about the health benefits of bone broth, because there is so much to know, and I am certainly not an expert. I do know that it is delicious and healthy, and I love it when I have a cold. I like to change up the seasonings slightly if I change the bones, but this is an area where your own experimentation will highlight your own personal preferences. Have fun with this one, and enjoy!

Makes about 6 Quarts

- bones - about 2-4 pounds of chicken bones or carcass | see beef variation below
- 8 quarts of cold water, or whatever your big pot holds | 6-12 quarts is good
- 2 tablespoons apple cider vinegar
- 1 onion, halved, not peeled
- 2 large carrots, washed
- 2 stalks celery, washed
- 2 tablespoons dried herbs | thyme, oregano, sage, dill, Italian seasoning
- 2 bay leaves
- 1 bunch fresh parsley, preferably flat leaf
- 1 tablespoon kosher salt
- 1 teaspoon black peppercorns

1. Put the bones, the cold water and the vinegar in a large pot and let it sit for about 4 hours. Make sure the water is nice and cold when you start.
2. Then, add all the other ingredients and cook over low, simmering and covered for 2-3 days.
3. Add more water when it decreases more than a quart or 2.
4. Strain out solids, taste for seasoning, add salt and pepper if desired and refrigerate or freeze until use.

Note:

To make beef bone broth, roast the bones at 400 degrees for about 45 minutes. Then paint them with tomato paste and roast for about 15 minutes longer. You can also use a slow cooker for the simmering. Cook on low, covered, for 2 days, and you don't need to fret about having something on your stove cooking for that long.

Fig Pecan Jam with Port

When I moved to California in 2007, one of the first things I did was buy a fig tree and plant it in my front yard. It's a small tree and only yields about 3 to 5 figs at a time, but they are beautiful and delicious! This recipe for fig-pecan jam with port is not as sweet as a regular jam, so it's absolutely lovely on a cheeseboard with dollops of goat cheese and baguette slices, truffle honey and hunks of parmigiano and slices of salami and prosciutto.

Makes 6-8 cups

- 4 pounds of figs, stems removed and coarsely chopped.
- ½ cups honey
- 1 ½ cups sugar
- 1 cups of toasted chopped pecans (optional)
- 2 tablespoons freshly squeezed lemon juice
- ¼ cups port, I like tawny port (optional)

1. Add the figs, honey, sugar, and lemon juice to a medium size saucepan.
2. Bring to a boil, lower heat and cook until thick; approximately 60 – 90 minutes, stirring frequently. If at this point it seems too chunky and thick for your taste, use an immersion blender, or regular blender or food processor to partially puree. Puree about 2 cups and add back into the pot.
3. Add the chopped pecans and port and cook for an additional 10 to 15 minutes, stirring often.
4. Let cool slightly and taste, to make sure you like the flavor, and adjust sugar, honey, lemon, nuts or port accordingly.
5. Pour hot jam into sterilized ½ pint jars, put on cap, screw band fingertip tight. Process filled jars in boiling water for 12 minutes. Let sit undisturbed overnight, and put the unsealed jars in the refrigerator.

Homemade Vanilla Extract

The majority of items I sell at the farmstand are baked goods, and all of it is made with my very own homemade vanilla extract! As it turns out, I use a little more than half a gallon a month as well as selling out of it weekly at the farmstand. Instead of using the typical method of making vanilla, I found that I love the flavor of bourbon and the lightness of the vodka and adore the flavor of them combined. This is such an easy recipe to make but requires one's patience and time. Your baking will be better for it!

Makes What Fits in Your Jar

- organic vanilla beans
- vodka
- bourbon

1. Use a clean jar with a nice airtight lid. A mason jar would be perfect. Use about five beans per pint. If you are making a quart jar, use 10 whole vanilla beans.

2. Put the beans in the clean jar, then fill it halfway with vodka and then the remaining with bourbon. Use a quality of alcohol that you would consider drinking, nothing cheap.

3. Gently shake and store in a dark cabinet that is cool and dry for about three months.

4. To accelerate this process, fine chop one of the beans instead of keeping it whole when you put the beans in the jar. This will take about a month off of the brewing time, reducing it to two months.

5. Shake it every couple of days when you think of it.

6. To use, simply spoon out how much you need. The alcohol will be vanilla flavored and scented and is absolutely amazing.

7. You can still use the vanilla bean seeds in recipes too, pull a bean out with clean hands, split open, and scrape the seeds out with a butter knife. They are so beautiful and delicious in a custard or ice cream.

NOTE:

This makes a great gift, just brew in a cute/fancy bottle.

Apricot Mustard

Urban Dreamer Farm & Vineyard
Auburn, CA 95603 urbandreamerfarm.org
REG # PR19647 Issued in Placer County

Apricot Mustard

Ingredients: apple cider vinegar, mustard seeds (brown & yellow), sugar, peaches, apricots, lemon and dried mustard

Net Wt 16 Oz. (454 grams)

MADE IN MY HOME KITCHEN

Apricot Mustard

One of my dearest friends, Susan, has a passion for mustard like no one I have ever known. It's not unusual at all for her to have 20 different kinds of mustard in her refrigerator at any time, and to find ways to incorporate it into her varied meals each and every day. I think of her with a smile absolutely every time I make this. Slightly spicy and a little fruity, this delicious and complex mustard is wonderful on meats, sandwiches, and mixed into your favorite vinaigrette for a salad.

Makes 2 Pints

- 1 pound fresh apricots
- ½ cup dried apricots
- ¾ cup sugar
- zest and juice of one lemon
- ½ cup yellow mustard seeds
- ½ cup brown mustard seeds
- 2 cups apple cider vinegar
- 1 tablespoon prepared Dijon mustard

1. Clean fresh apricots and remove the pit. Leave the skin on. Put them in a saucepan big enough to eventually hold all the ingredients.
2. Add dried apricots, lemon zest and juice and sugar. Warm slowly on the stove until the sugar melts and the fresh apricots start to disintegrate and the dried apricots soften.
3. Turn off the heat, put a lid on, and let sit until cool. Once cool, purée to desired level of chunkiness using a blender, immersion blender or a food processor.
4. Let sit with the lid on until the mustard seeds are ready.
5. Meanwhile, grind the mustard seeds coarsely and put in glass measuring cups or a bowl. I recommend using a spice grinder for this or a mortar and pestle. I've tried this in the blender and food processor also, and it never goes well. The seeds need to crack open to release their amazing flavor, but also still have the telltale grainy texture.
6. Pour the apple cider vinegar and tablespoon of Dijon mustard over the ground seeds, stir to combine, cover with plastic, and let sit for 8 hours or overnight.
7. Stir the mustard seed and vinegar mixture into the apricot mixture in a pot and warm over low heat, stirring often, until hot.
8. It will thicken as it cooks. Once it reaches your desired consistency, it's ready.
9. Store in a clean jar in the refrigerator for months or can with the water bath method for dry storage.

✎ NOTE:

This makes a great gift and is also quite versatile. For more fruit flavor, double the amount of apricot and sugar. To alter the consistency, more grainy or smooth, just adjust how much you grind the seeds.

Farmstand Guacamole

Are you a customer of the Farmstand? I know some of you will buy this book just to get your hands on my tried-and-true guacamole recipe. I understand, it's my absolute favorite thing too and I couldn't make this cookbook without including this recipe!

Serves 4

- 4-5 avocados
- 2 teaspoons lime juice, freshly squeezed
- ½ teaspoon dried minced onion or dried minced shallot
- 1 teaspoon finely chopped garlic
- ¼ teaspoon dried ground coriander
- 1 teaspoon kosher salt
- ½ cup (or more to taste) chopped cilantro
- ½ cup chopped fresh tomato (a good one) or cherry tomato

1. Put the lime juice, dried minced onion, chopped garlic and coriander into the bottom of the bowl and let sit for a few minutes.

2. Meanwhile, peel and pit the avocados and put them into the bowl on top of the lime juice mixture. Add the salt and combine the avocados with the lime juice mixture and the salt with a pastry blender two butter knives, cutting through the avocado so that you still have nice big chunks of avocado.

3. Add the cilantro and the tomato and stir gently.

4. Taste. Add more salt, lime juice, and / or cilantro until the flavor is what you like.

Spicy Pickled Green Beans

This recipe is an old family favorite. It's such a great use for those fresh green beans from a community garden, your own backyard or farmers' market.

Makes about 2 Pints

- 30 to 40 fresh, young "Kentucky Wonder" pole beans or any fresh green beans
- ½ teaspoon red pepper
- 1-2 cloves garlic
- 1 head fresh heads dill weed
- ½ cup cider vinegar
- ½ cup water
- salt

1. Sterilize pint jars and tops and vertically pack beans.
2. To each pint, add ½ teaspoon red pepper, 1 or 2 cloves garlic, and 1 head of fresh dill.
3. For each pint, bring to a boil a solution of ½ cups cider vinegar, ½ cups water, and 1 tablespoon salt.
4. Fill jars of beans with boiling solution and seal at once, preferably in a boiling water bath for 5 minutes. Do not open for at least 3 weeks.
5. Serve as an hors d'oeuvre or condiment. Serves 10.

✎ NOTE:

Add as a garnish to a Bloody Mary. Place 2-3 green beans in the glass and enjoy!

Bread & Butter Pickles

It's hard not to think of long lazy summer days when I taste bread and butter pickles. Cheeseburgers on the grill. Grandma's potato salad. Fresh sliced home-grown summer tomatoes. The sound of the screen door flapping open and closed as little feet wander in and outside again.

Makes 5 pints

- 10 cups sliced trimmed cucumbers about a quarter inch thick, I use English hothouse cucumbers, but any pickling cucumber would work fine
- 3 medium onions thinly sliced
- ½ cup kosher salt
- 1 cup white vinegar
- 2 cups apple cider vinegar
- 1 cup sugar
- 1 cup brown sugar
- 2 tablespoons mustard seeds
- 1 teaspoon celery seeds
- 1 teaspoon ground turmeric
- 1 teaspoon ground ginger

1. In a glass or stainless-steel bowl, combine cucumbers, onions and salt. Mix well, cover with cold water and let stand at room temperature for two hours or up to six hours.

2. Transfer to a colander placed over the sink and rinse with cold running water and drain thoroughly.

3. In a large stainless-steel saucepan, combine vinegars, sugars, mustard seeds, celery seeds, turmeric, and ginger.

4. Bring to a boil over medium high heat, stirring to dissolve the sugars.

5. Stir in the cucumbers and return to boil. You will see the cucumbers transition from bright green to more yellow-green.

6. Preserve for the pantry by hot canning, or simply put them in clean containers and keep in the refrigerator.

Balsamic Onions

The first time I ate balsamic onions was in Italy. They were served with braised rabbit and handmade pasta for lunch and completely stole the show. Sweet, sour, salty and tender, I couldn't wait to get home and figure out how to replicate that incredible taste. This recipe is my take on those amazing onions!

The use of frozen pearl onions in this recipe is a gigantic time saver. You should be able to purchase frozen pearl onions at your grocery store. The balsamic vinegar you use in this recipe will impart the more important part of the flavor. I recommend using the best you can find locally, but nothing older than 12 years... that's something that should be savored!

Makes 2 Pints

- 2 14-ounce bags frozen pearl onions
- ½ cups white wine vinegar
- 1 ½ cups aged or relatively good balsamic vinegar, not older than 12 years
- ½ cup water
- 2 teaspoons kosher salt
- 1/3 cup sugar
- 1 teaspoon peppercorns
- 3-4 bay leaves

NOTE:

Pair these with rich meats, wild game and long braises, or chop whole in salads.

1. Prepare your jars for canning, make sure they are clean and hot and have any other canning tools ready.

2. Thaw the onions and place them in your jars, about 3-4 half pint jars, making sure there is ½ inch headspace in the jar.

3. Divide all the peppercorns and bay leaves evenly between the jars.

4. Meanwhile, heat the vinegars and water in a glass bowl or measuring cups in the microwave until hot. Stir in the sugar and salt until it dissolves.

5. Pour the brine (the vinegar mixture) over the onions in the jars, making sure there is a ½ inch headspace in the jars. Place the clean, hot lids and rings. I like to have them ready, submerged in a glass measuring cups of boiling water onto the jars.

6. Only tighten the rings to fingertip tightness. Tightening them too much will not allow the steam to escape and they won't seal.

7. Process in a water or steam bath canner for 15 minutes.

8. Place any jars that don't seal into the refrigerator. They should last at least 2 months, and sealed jars can be stored in your cool dark cabinet for up to 18 months. The flavor improves with time.

Tuna Fish with Pickled Red Onions & Pepitas

Sometimes I crave the most basic things more than the fanciest most delicious dinner or dessert you could imagine. Tuna is one of those things from time to time. I like it for a snack or a lunch about once every month or two and find it so satisfying. Enjoy it over pasta, either warm or cold, with crackers, with cucumber rounds, or on a sandwich or open faced as a melt spread on toast, with your favorite cheese melted on top!

Serves 2

- 10 ounces high quality, canned tuna, drained
- ¼ cup mayonnaise
- salt and pepper to taste
- 2 tablespoons chopped pepitas, toasted or roasted salted
- 2 tablespoons pickled red onions, chopped fine

Pickled Red Onions

- 1 large red onion, peeled and sliced
- 1 ½ cups water
- 1 cup white vinegar or if you prefer – red wine vinegar or apple cider vinegar
- 2 tablespoons kosher salt
- 2 tablespoons sugar
- 1 bay laurel leaf
- 6 whole peppercorns or black peppercorns

1. Place the onion, bay leaf and peppercorns into a 4 cups container that has a lid and can be stored in the refrigerator.

2. In a separate container, heat the water in the microwave until hot. Stir in the salt and sugar until it dissolves.

3. Add the vinegar to the water. Pour the hot liquid over the onion mixture and let sit on the counter until cool.

4. Place on the cover and refrigerate until you are ready to use it. Wait at least 2 hours for the onions to pickle before using. They should be kept in the refrigerator for 2 weeks or longer.

5. In a medium bowl, mix the tuna, mayonnaise, pepitas, pickled red onions and salt and pepper to taste. Serve immediately!

✎ NOTE:

Modify by swapping the pickled red onion for pickle relish and the pepitas for toasted sunflower seeds.

Fresh Garlic Dill Pickles

Fresh pickles have always been a love of my whole family. This recipe is so simple. It's important to have fresh ingredients. If your dried dill has been in your cabinet for over a year, consider a new bottle.

Makes 4 Quarts

- 14-16 cups of cucumbers sliced thick, to fill 4 quarts. I don't peel them, but you certainly can. Make sure they are clean and mold free.
- If you want to avoid any bitterness, taste a slice from each cucumber as you are filling your containers. Discard the bitter cucumbers (the whole cucumber).
- 4 garlic cloves, peeled
- 4 tablespoons dried dill (or double the amount of fresh if you have it)
- 2 cups apple cider vinegar (organic if possible) 1/3 cups Kosher salt
- 6 cups water

1. Heat the water in a large glass 8-cups measuring cups or bowl in the microwave till boiling, about 4 minutes on high should do it.
2. Meanwhile, divide the cucumbers between 4 1-quart containers. In each container, place 1 tablespoon of dill and one clove of garlic.
3. Once the water is hot, remove it from the microwave, stir in the salt until dissolved. Mix in the vinegar, and then pour the water-salt-vinegar mixture over the cucumbers into your quart containers.
4. Let cool slightly, then put the lids on and put in the refrigerator.
5. Enjoy as soon as the next day, these pickles make wonderful gifts.
6. To ensure freshness, keep fingers out of the pickles. They should be good for a month.

Habanero Apricot Jelly

This is the most popular jelly at my farmstand. I probably sell about as much as this jelly as all the other jams and jellies combined. Customers love to serve it on appetizer platters, and they give it as gifts. The most common way to serve it is on cream cheese or goat cheese with crackers. The luscious orange and bright red of the ingredients make it truly beautiful to look at. It is truly spectacular! The spiciness is instant but is immediately followed by a very fruity sweet tang from the apricot and the peaches.

Makes a lot

- 4 cups cleaned pitted sliced peaches
- 4 ½ cups white vinegar
- 3 cups chopped dried apricots
- 7 ½ pounds of sugar
- 2 medium red bell peppers, chopped
- 2 medium onions, chopped
- 2 cups stemmed roughly chopped habanero peppers, for less heat, remove some of the seeds
- 2 large apples, cleaned, quartered, and cored

1. Add all the ingredients to a large pot and stir together over medium-high heat until all of the ingredients have softened.

2. Puree using an immersion blender or putting batches into your blender being very careful not to overfill as the ingredients will be hot and you don't want them to splatter.

3. Return everything to the pot and continue to boil, stirring constantly until the jelly is the consistency that you like.

4. Keep a plate or a dish in the freezer and keep testing it until you like the way it tastes and the way it sets up. Some people prefer a thinner jelly and some prefer a thicker jelly. If it doesn't seem to be thickening enough for you, add ½ cup of sugar, stir to dissolve, and boil, stirring constantly, until it reaches the consistency you like.

5. While it is still hot, ladle the jelly into hot clean jars and continue to follow hot water canning guidelines to preserve in jars. I typically process for 15 minutes.

Pineapple Jalapeno Jelly

My goodness, how do I explain how delicious this recipe smells when you are cooking? To me, it smells like Hawaii. One spoonful of this stirred into your salsa gives it a tropical essence. A spoonful stirred into avocado corn and black beans makes a delightful topping for fish. A spoonful stirred into your margarita makes it a pineapple jalapeno margarita. And finally, a spoonful of this with a chunk of goat cheese or cream cheese and crackers makes a very lovely appetizer.

Makes a lot

- 3 pounds peeled, cored, cleaned fresh or frozen pineapple
- 4 ½ cups white vinegar
- 7 ½ pounds sugar
- 2 medium yellow or orange bell peppers, chopped
- 2 medium onions chopped
- 3 cups stemmed roughly chopped jalapeno peppers, for less heat, remove some of the seeds
- 2 large apples, cleaned, quartered, and cored

1. Add all the ingredients to a large pot and stir together over medium-high heat until all of the ingredients have softened.

2. Puree using an immersion blender or putting batches into your blender being very careful not to overfill as the ingredients will be hot and you don't want them to splatter.

3. Return everything to the pot and continue to boil, stirring constantly until the jelly is the consistency that you like.

4. Keep a plate or a dish in the freezer and keep testing it until you like the way it tastes and the way it sets up. Some people prefer a thinner jelly and some prefer a thicker jelly. If it doesn't seem to be thickening enough for you, add ½ cup of sugar, stir to dissolve, and boil, stirring constantly, until it reaches the consistency you like.

5. While it is still hot, ladle the jelly into hot clean jars and continue to follow hot water canning guidelines to preserve in jars. I typically process for 15 minutes.

Super Elderberry Syrup

Years ago, a dear friend told me about the elderberry and how it can help to boost the immune system, because it's packed with antioxidants and vitamins. She suggested that I could make a syrup on the cook top in about 30 minutes that would aid in helping to keep my family healthy and ward off illness. I went immediately to the store to buy all the ingredients plus a few more that I thought would be beneficial and help with the flavor. I've been making this for my farmstand ever since and have had many very happy and healthy customers.

Makes 7 pints

- 1 cup dried elderberries
- 2 tablespoons dried echinacea
- 2 star anise
- 8 cloves
- 1 3-inch cinnamon stick
- ½ cup of dried blueberries
- 1 tablespoon dried ashwagandha
- 1 tablespoon dried astragalus root
- 1 tablespoon dried goldenseal
- 1 tablespoon dried stinging nettles
- 1 tablespoon dried ginger
- 1 3-inch piece dried red reishi mushroom
- 4 quarts water
- 1-2 cups good honey

1. Put all the dried ingredients and the water into a large pot on the stove and simmer at medium to low heat for one hour, cool slightly. Maybe about 30 minutes, and then strain through a sign mesh strainer.

2. Stir one cup of honey into the strained liquid. Taste to make sure that you like it and add more honey until it tastes acceptable to you.

3. Store in clean jars in the refrigerator and use within a month or can with the water bath method for dry storage.

NOTE:

when you make this syrup with local raw honey (which has its own list of health benefits) and preserve using US canning methods, you lose the allergy and immune boosting benefits you get from the honey, but still preserve the delicious flavor.

Peach Bourbon Barbecue Sauce

I love this BBQ sauce. It reminds me of something you would want to drink with a straw. The smell is so intoxicating you will want to make it again and again.

Makes a lot

- 3 pounds cleaned, pitted, quartered peaches, fresh or frozen
- 2 medium onions, peeled and quartered
- 1 cup bourbon
- ¼ cup olive oil
- 1 tablespoon smoked paprika
- 3 garlic cloves, crushed
- 1 ½ cups apple cider vinegar
- 1 ½ cups brown sugar
- 1 #10 can diced tomatoes in their juice. These are the very large, over 100 ounces, cans you can find at some grocery stores. If you cannot find one, use 7 of the 14-15 ounce cans of diced tomatoes
- 2 tablespoons dried mustard
- 3 tablespoons Dijon mustard
- 3 tablespoons Worcestershire sauce
- 1 tablespoon salt
- 1 teaspoon ground black pepper
- 1 tablespoon urfa biber chile, dried - optional, available at specialty markets and online. Urfa biber is from Turkey and it's slightly spicy, smokey and super delicious
- 1 tablespoon Aleppo pepper chile dried - optional, available at specialty markets and online. Aleppo pepper is from Syria and it is a little bit lighter and spicier
- 1 ½ teaspoons cayenne pepper

1. Line a large cookie sheet with foil and spray with cooking spray. Scatter the peaches and onions on the pan.
2. Broil under the broiler in the oven for 10 to 15 minutes until slightly caramelized. Ideally it will be dark brown or black but not burnt on the corners. Set aside until later.
3. Pour the olive oil into the bottom of a large saucepan over medium heat.
4. Add the paprika, garlic, and cook stirring constantly for one minute.
5. Stir in the vinegar and brown sugar and cook for 2-3 minutes or until syrupy.
6. Stir in the can of diced tomatoes and the juice, mustard, Worcestershire sauce, salt, pepper, dried chili powders, cayenne pepper, and broiled peaches and onions.
7. Bring to a simmer, cover, and cook for 30 minutes, stirring occasionally.
8. Remove the lid, add the bourbon, and cook uncovered for 10-15 minutes, stirring often.
9. Remove from heat, cool slightly.
10. Process the sauce in a blender until very smooth. Return to the saucepan, bring to a boil. Taste.
11. Adjust the seasonings to your palate.
12. The sauce is ready. Store in clean jars in the refrigerator and use within a month or can with the water bath method for dry storage.

✎ Note:

This BBQ sauce is actually quite delicious when you replace the peaches with cherries. To do this, omit the peaches. Instead, add two cups of dried tart cherries with the bourbon at the end.

Moroccan Chickpea Stew

This recipe ALMOST didn't make it into this cookbook. As much as I adore this stew, it just plain slipped my mind until a handful of customers gasped that they couldn't wait to get their hands on it after hearing about this cookbook coming out. My immediate reaction was panic and then I immediately added it in! The warm spices and luscious tomatoes are a perfect balance for the hearty chickpeas, carrots and potatoes. Everything is enhanced by the greens and sweet potatoes in this plant based delicious soup.

Serves 4-6

- 1 tablespoon extra-virgin olive oil
- 1 medium onion, chopped
- 3 large carrots, chopped
- ½ pound sweet potatoes, cubed, wash and leave the skins on
- ½ pound gold potatoes, cubed wash and leave the skins on
- saffron, a small pinch, about 10 threads, ground between fingers
- 1 teaspoon ground smoked paprika
- 1 teaspoon ground cumin
- 1 teaspoon minced garlic
- salt and pepper to taste
- 4 cups vegetable broth
- 1-24 ounce can chickpeas (garbanzo beans), rinsed and drained
- 1-24 ounce canned diced tomatoes
- 10 ounces power greens (combination of kale, spinach and Swiss chard)
- juice of one lemon

1. Put the oil in a large pot on the stove over medium heat. Add onion, carrot, sweet potato, gold potato and spices and cook until onions are slightly translucent on the edges and no longer look raw.

2. Add broth, chickpeas, and canned tomatoes and cook until potatoes and carrots are tender.

3. With an immersion blender or potato masher, slightly puree the soup to thicken it. It should still be mostly whole chopped veggies and chick peas.

4. Stir in the greens and cook until wilted and darker in color, about 5 minutes.

5. Add the lemon juice and taste for seasoning. Add salt or pepper if needed. Enjoy!

NOTE:

For a thinner stew, add some additional water or broth. For a little heat, add a pinch of ground cayenne pepper and crushed red pepper with the other spices.

White Chicken Chili

This chili has become a solid staple of the Urban Dreamer Farmstand over the years. It's creamy and has no dairy or soy in it at all. Its thick and chunky and flavorful, and my favorite way to enjoy this chili is in a shallow bowl with a fried egg on top. It's also so lovely with a spoonful of plain yogurt stirred in. It becomes creamy and tangy and so delicious in a new way.

Serves 4

- 1 medium yellow onion, chopped
- 1 teaspoon minced garlic
- 1 tablespoon vegetable or canola oil or other light oil you prefer
- ½ pound poblano peppers, diced in ½ inch chunks
- 2 jalapeno peppers, minced
- 1 pound gold potatoes, diced in ½ inch chunks
- 1-12 ounce jar salsa verde
- 1 teaspoon ground cumin
- 1 teaspoon ground coriander
- salt and pepper to taste
- 1 quart chicken broth
- 2- 24 ounce cans white beans, rinsed and drained
- 1-pound cooked chopped chicken
- juice of one Lime
- 3 tablespoons chopped fresh cilantro

1. Put the oil in a large pot on the stove over medium heat. Add onion, garlic, poblano peppers, jalapeno peppers, potatoes, salsa verde, and spices.
2. Cook until the onions soften slightly and no longer look raw.
3. Puree the chicken broth with one of the cans of beans and add to the pot.
4. Add the chicken and the other can of beans. If the liquid doesn't cover everything, add a splash more water or chicken broth until the vegetables and chicken are slightly submerged.
5. Simmer on low until the potatoes and peppers are tender.
6. Add the lime juice and cilantro and taste for seasoning. Enjoy!

Index

A

acini di pepe, 52
alcohol
- bourbon (See bourbon)
- brandy, 151-152
- cognac (See cognac)
- port, 203
- sherry (See sherry)
- vermouth, 93, 146
- vodka, 204-206
- whiskey, 193-195 (See also bourbon)
- wine (See wine, red; wine, white)

Aleppo pepper, 218-219
almonds
- California Slaw, 107
- Celery Apple Salad, 117
- Peanut Butter Toffee, 174-175

Ancho chilies, 43
anchovies, 146-147
andouille, 142
apple cider
- Apple Cider Donut Cupcakes, 32
- Green Smoothie, 95

Apple Cider Donut Cupcakes, 32
Apple Dutch Baby, 25
apples
- Apple Dutch Baby, 25
- Celery Apple Salad, 117
- Choucroute Garnie, 84
- Green Smoothie, 95
- Habanero Apricot Jelly, 215
- Pineapple Jalapeno Jelly, 216

applesauce, 32
apricot jam/jelly, 82
Apricot Mustard, 207
apricots
- Apricot Mustard, 207
- Habanero Apricot Jelly, 215

arborio rice, 139-143
Artichokes, 144
arugula, 113
ashwagandha, 217
asparagus, 35
astragalus root, 217
avocados
- California Slaw, 107
- Farmstand Guacamole, 209

Award-winning Shrimp Pad Thai, 83

B

bacon
- Beef Burgundy, 151-152
- Broccoli Bacon Carbonara, 52
- California Slaw, 107
- Crab Omelet, 132-133
- Orecchiette, 55
- Quiche Lorraine, 134-135
- in Risotto, 141

Balsamic Onions, 212
bananas
- Breakfast Cupcakes, 29
- Green Smoothie, 95

barbecue sauce, 218-219
bars
- Keto Lemon Bars, 187
- Keto Pumpkin Bars, 190
- Lemon Bars, 186

beans
- black, 70-71
- cannellini, 56-57
- garbanzo/chickpeas, 113, 220-221
- green, 85-87, 146-147, 210
- white, 223

bechamel sauce, 49
beef
- Beef Burgundy, 151-152
- Bolognese Sauce & Lasagna Bolognese, 48-49
- Enchiladas, 75
- Filet Mignon with Bordelaise, 127
- in Risotto, 140
- Short Ribs, 129
- Skirt Steak, 73

Beef Burgundy, 151-152
beets
- Butternut Squash & Roasted Fall Vegetable Soup, 90-91
- Post Chuck E. Cheese Recovery Salad, 110-111

bell peppers
- Habanero Apricot Jelly, 215
- Panzanella, 112
- Pineapple Jalapeno Jelly, 216

Berry Bran Muffins, 26
black beans, 70-71
blackberries, 26
blueberries
- Berry Bran Muffins, 26
- Blueberry Scones, 31
- Super Elderberry Syrup, 217

Blueberry Scones, 31

blue cheese, 142
Bolognese Sauce, 48-49
Bone Broth, 202
bouillabaisse, 148-149
bourbon
- Brown Butter Bourbon Pecan Pie, 164-165
- Chocolate Whiskey Cupcakes with Salted Whiskey Caramel Frosting (gluten free), 193-195
- Homemade Vanilla Extract, 204-206
- Peach Bourbon Barbecue Sauce, 218-219

brandy, 151-152
Bread & Butter Pickles, 211
breads. See also muffins
- Blueberry Scones, 31
- Challah Bread, 21
- Focaccia, 200-201
- Panzanella, 112

Breakfast Cupcakes, 29
breakfasts
- Apple Cider Donut Cupcakes, 32
- Apple Dutch Baby, 25
- Berry Bran Muffins, 26
- Breakfast Cupcakes, 29
- Challah Bread, 21
- Crab Omelet, 132-133
- Granola, 18
- Quiche Lorraine, 134-135
- Roasted Asparagus with Soft Cooked Eggs, 35
- Scones, 31
- Zucchini Bread Cupcakes, 23

Brie cheese, 142
broccoli
- Broccoli Bacon Carbonara, 52
- Broccoli Cheese Soup, 118
- in Risotto, 142

Broccoli Bacon Carbonara, 52
Broccoli Cheese Soup, 118
broccolini, in Risotto, 141
Brown Butter Bourbon Pecan Pie, 164-165
Brulé Topping, 180-182
Brussels sprouts, 55
Butterflied Leg of Lamb, 153
Butternut Squash & Roasted Fall Vegetable Soup, 90-91
butter sauce, 64-65

C

cabbage
- Award-winning Shrimp Pad Thai, 83
- California Slaw, 107
- Pregnancy Salad, a.k.a. Hot Summer Night Tuna Salad, 114
- Ribollita - Tuscan White Bean and Vegetable Stew, 56-57
- Sriracha, 70-71

cakes, 176-177. See also cupcakes, dessert
California Slaw, 107
cannellini beans, 56-57
capers, 146-147
caprese-style risotto, 140
caramel, salted, 170-171, 194
carbonara, 52
carbonara-style risotto, 141
Carrot Cake Cupcakes, 162-163
Carrot Puree, 105
carrots
- Beef Burgundy, 151-152
- Bolognese Sauce, 48-49
- Bone Broth, 202
- Broccoli Cheese Soup, 118
- Butternut Squash & Roasted Fall Vegetable Soup, 90-91
- Carrot Cake Cupcakes, 162-163
- Carrot Puree, 105
- Chicken and Dumplings, 68-69
- Chicken Pot Pie, 85-87
- Moroccan Chickpea Stew, 220-221
- New Mexico Green Chili Stew with Chicken, 93
- Osso Buco, 125
- Ribollita - Tuscan White Bean and Vegetable Stew, 56-57
- in Risotto, 141

cauliflower
- in Risotto, 142
- Roasted Cauliflower, 102

celery
- Bolognese Sauce, 48-49
- Bone Broth, 202
- Celery Apple Salad, 117
- Chicken and Dumplings, 68-69
- Chicken Pot Pie, 85-87
- Green Smoothie, 95
- Osso Buco, 125
- Panzanella, 112
- Quinoa Salad, 113
- Ribollita - Tuscan White Bean and Vegetable Stew, 56-57

Celery Apple Salad, 117
Challah Bread, 21
cheddar cheese
- Broccoli Cheese Soup, 118
- Crab Omelet, 132-133
- Enchilada Sauce, 70-71
- in Risotto, 142

Cheesecake, 183
cheesecake, Keto, 191
cheeses
- blue, 142
- Brie, 142
- cheddar (See cheddar cheese)
- gruyere, 134-135
- havarti, 142
- Monterey Jack, 76-77

- mozzarella, 80-81
- parmesan (See parmesan cheese)
- parmigiano or pecorino, 35
- ricotta, 80-81
- shredded, 70-71

chia seeds, 18

chicken
- Chicken and Dumplings, 68-69
- Chicken Bouillabaisse with Rouille, 148-149
- Chicken Pot Pie, 85-87
- Chicken Tenderloins with White Wine Butter Sauce, 64-65
- Fennel Chicken, 62
- Fried Chicken, 63
- Green Chicken Enchiladas, 76-77
- liver, for Bolognese Sauce, 48-49
- New Mexico Green Chili Stew with Chicken, 93
- Vacation Chicken, 66-67
- White Chicken Chili, 223

Chicken and Dumplings, 68-69
Chicken Bouillabaisse with Rouille, 148-149
Chicken Pot Pie, 85-87
Chicken Tenderloins with White Wine Butter Sauce, 64-65

chickpeas/garbanzo beans
- Moroccan Chickpea Stew, 220-221
- Quinoa Salad, 113

chili, white chicken, 223

chilies. See also peppers
- Ancho, 43
- green, canned, 76-77, 141
- Hatch (NM) red powder, 74
- New Mexico green, 93
- Urfa biber, 218-219

chocolate
- Breakfast Cupcakes, 29
- Chocolate Whiskey Cupcakes with Salted Whiskey Caramel Frosting (gluten free), 193-195
- Flourless Chocolate Cake (gluten free), 176-177
- French Silk Pie, 185
- German Chocolate Cupcakes, 160-161
- Peanut Butter Toffee, 174-175
- Pots de Crème (gluten free), 179
- Salted Chocolate Chip Cookies (gluten free, vegan), 173

Chocolate Whiskey Cupcakes with Salted Whiskey Caramel Frosting (gluten free), 193-195
Choucroute Garnie, 84
Coconut-Pecan Filling, 160-161

cognac
- Chicken Tenderloins with White Wine Butter Sauce, 64-65
- Escargot, 138
- Pots de Crème (gluten free), 179

collagen hydrolysate powder, 33

- Composed Niçoise Salad, 146-147

condiments. See also dressings; sauces
- Apricot Mustard, 207
- barbecue sauce, 218-219
- bechamel sauce, 49
- Habanero Apricot Jelly, 215
- honey (See honey)
- jams/jellies (See jams/jellies)

cookies, 173

corn
- New Mexico Green Chili Stew with Chicken, 93
- in Risotto, 141

crab
- Crab Omelet, 132-133
- in Risotto, 140

Crab Omelet, 132-133
Cream Cheese Buttercream Frosting, 163, 188-189
Cream of Tomato Soup, 89
Crispy Chinese Roasted Duck, 130-131

cucumbers
- Bread & Butter Pickles, 211
- California Slaw, 107
- Fresh Garlic Dill Pickles, 214
- Green Smoothie, 95
- Quinoa Salad, 113

cupcakes, breakfast. See muffins

cupcakes, dessert
- Carrot Cake Cupcakes, 162-163
- Chocolate Whiskey Cupcakes with Salted Whiskey Caramel Frosting (gluten free), 193-195
- German Chocolate Cupcakes, 160-161
- Lemon Lemon Cupcakes, 188-189

custard
- Custard & Custard Pie, 166-167
- Spiced Pear Custard Brulé Pie, 180-182

Custard & Custard Pie, 166-167

D

dates, 142
dill, 214

dressings
- for California Slaw, 107
- Tangy Mustard Vinaigrette, 111, 146
- Vinaigrette, 109

dried fruit. See fruit, dried

drinks
- Green Smoothie, 95
- Warm & Satisfying Eggnog, 33

drupes. See nuts/drupes
duck, 130-131
dumplings, 68-69
Dutch baby, 25

E

echinacea, 217
eggnog, 33
eggplant
- Even Better, BEST Spaghetti Sauce, 46
- Ratatouille, 103

eggs
- Composed Niçoise Salad, 146-147
- Crab Omelet, 132-133
- Fresh Pasta, 40-41
- Quiche Lorraine, 134-135
- Roasted Asparagus with Soft Cooked Eggs, 35
- Warm & Satisfying Eggnog, 33

elderberries, 217
Enchiladas, 75
enchiladas, green chicken, 76-77
Enchilada Sauce, 74
endive, Belgian, 110-111
Escargot, 138
espresso, 160-161
Even Better, BEST Spaghetti Sauce, 46

F

Farmstand Guacamole, 209
Fennel Chicken, 62
Fig Pecan Jam with Port, 203
Filet Mignon with Bordelaise, 127
Fish Tacos, 70-71
flaxseed meal, 173
Flourless Chocolate Cake (gluten free), 176-177
Focaccia, 200-201
French Fries, 101
French Potato Salad, 146
French Silk Pie, 185
Fresh Garlic Dill Pickles, 214
Fresh Pasta, 40-41
Fried Chicken, 63
frosting
- Cream Cheese Buttercream Frosting, 163, 188-189
- Salted Whiskey Caramel, 194

fruit, dried
- Blueberry Scones, 31
- Granola, 18
- Super Elderberry Syrup, 217

G

garbanzo beans/chickpeas
- Moroccan Chickpea Stew, 220-221
- Quinoa Salad, 113

garlic
- Fresh Garlic Dill Pickles, 214
- Garlic Soup, 106

Garlic Soup, 106

German chocolate, Pots de Crème (gluten free), 179
German Chocolate Cupcakes, 160-161
gluten-free dishes. See also Keto recipes
- Chocolate Whiskey Cupcakes with Salted Whiskey Caramel Frosting, 193-194
- Flourless Chocolate Cake, with modification, 176-177
- Green Chicken Enchiladas, with modification, 76-77
- Keto Cheesecake, 191
- Keto Pumpkin Bars, 190
- Pots de Crème, 179
- Salted Chocolate Chip Cookies, 173
- Vacation Chicken, with modification, 66-67

goldenseal, 217
graham cracker crumbs
- Cheesecake, 183
- Peanut Butter Toffee, 174-175

Granola, 18
green beans
- Chicken Pot Pie, 85-87
- Composed Niçoise Salad, 146-147
- Spicy Pickled Green Beans, 210

Green Chicken Enchiladas, 76-77
green chilies, canned, 76-77, 141
greens. See individual greens
Green Smoothie, 95
Green Tea Ice Cream, 169
gruyere cheese, 134-135
guacamole, 209

H

Habanero Apricot Jelly, 215
Hatch, NM red chili powder, 74
havarti cheese, 142
hazelnuts, 55
Homemade Vanilla Extract, 204-206
hominy, 93
honey
- Challah Bread, 21
- Fig Pecan Jam with Port, 203
- Super Elderberry Syrup, 217
- Tangy Mustard Vinaigrette, 111, 146
- Vinaigrette, 109

I

ice cream, 169
ingredients, finding quality, 10-12

J

jalapeno peppers
- Green Chicken Enchiladas, 76-77
- Oven Roasted Spaghetti Sauce, 43

- Pineapple Jalapeno Jelly, 216
- White Chicken Chili, 223

jams/jellies
- Fig Pecan Jam with Port, 203
- Habanero Apricot Jelly, 215
- Pineapple Jalapeno Jelly, 216
- in Slow Cooker Turkey Breast, 82

K

kale
- Green Smoothie, 95
- Kale and Sausage Pie, 80-81
- Moroccan Chickpea Stew, 220-221
- Ribollita - Tuscan White Bean and Vegetable Stew, 56-57
- in Risotto, 142

Kale and Sausage Pie, 80-81
Keto Cheesecake, 191
Keto Lemon Bars, 187
Keto Pumpkin Bars, 190
kiwi, 110-111

L

lamb, 153
Lasagna Bolognese, 51
Lemon Bars, 186
lemon juice/zest
- Apricot Mustard, 207
- Artichokes, 144
- Beef Burgundy, 151-152
- Butterflied Leg of Lamb, 153
- Celery Apple Salad, 117
- Chicken Bouillabaisse with Rouille, 149
- Fig Pecan Jam with Port, 203
- Green Smoothie, 95
- Keto Lemon Bars, 187
- Lemon Bars, 186
- Lemon Lemon Cupcakes, 188-189
- Moroccan Chickpea Stew, 220-221
- Quinoa Salad, 113
- in Risotto, 143
- Spiced Pear Custard Brulé Pie, 180-182
- Tangy Mustard Vinaigrette, 111
- Vinaigrette, 109

Lemon Lemon Cupcakes, 188-189
Lemon Syrup, 189
lettuce. See also other greens
- Celery Apple Salad, 117
- Composed Niçoise Salad, 146-147

lime juice/zest
- Farmstand Guacamole, 209
- Nectarine Pie, 158-159
- New Mexico Green Chili Stew with Chicken, 93
- Quick Pickled Onions, 70-71
- White Chicken Chili, 223

liquor/liqueur. See alcohol
liver, 48-49
lobster, 140

M

macadamia nuts, 18
Magic Spaghetti Sauce, 46
mandarin oranges, 110-111
mangoes, 95
matcha green tea powder, 169
Monterey Jack cheese, 76-77
Moroccan Chickpea Stew, 220-221
mozzarella cheese, 80-81
muffins
- Apple Cider Donut Cupcakes, 32
- Berry Bran Muffins, 26
- Breakfast Cupcakes, 29
- Zucchini Bread Cupcakes, 23

mushrooms
- Beef Burgundy, 151-152
- in Risotto, 140, 142
- Super Elderberry Syrup, 217

mustard
- Apricot Mustard, 207
- Tangy Mustard Vinaigrette, 111

N

Nectarine Pie, 158-159
New Mexico Green Chili Stew with Chicken, 93
niçoise salad, 146-147
nut butter. See peanut butter
nuts/drupes
- almonds, 107, 117, 174-175
- hazelnuts, 55
- mixed, 18
- peanut, 83
- pecans (See pecans)
- pistachios, 18

O

oats, 18
olives, niçoise, 146-147
omelets, 132-133
onions. See also pearl onions
- Balsamic, 212
- pickled, 70-71, 213

orecchiette, 55
Osso Buco, 125
Oven Roasted Spaghetti Sauce, 43
Oysters Adrienne, 137

P

pad thai, 83
Panzanella, 112
parmesan cheese
- Broccoli Bacon Carbonara, 52
- Lasagna Bolognese, 51
- Pasta with Brussels Sprouts, 55
- in Risotto, 143

parmigiano cheese, 35
pasta. See also sauces
- Broccoli Bacon Carbonara, 52
- Fresh Pasta, 40–41
- Lasagna Bolognese, 51
- Pasta with Brussels Sprouts, 55
- Pregnancy Salad, a.k.a. Hot Summer Night Tuna Salad, 114

Pasta with Brussels Sprouts, 55
Peach Bourbon Barbecue Sauce, 218–219
peaches
- Green Smoothie, 95
- Habanero Apricot Jelly, 215
- Peach Bourbon Barbecue Sauce, 218–219

peanut butter
- Breakfast Cupcakes, 29
- Peanut Butter Toffee, 174–175
- powder, in Warm & Satisfying Eggnog, 33

Peanut Butter Toffee, 174–175
peanuts, 83
pearl onions
- Balsamic Onions, 212
- Beef Burgundy, 151–152
- in Risotto, 212

pears, 180–182
peas
- California Slaw, 107
- Chicken and Dumplings, 68–69
- Chicken Pot Pie, 85–87
- in Risotto, 140, 141, 143

pecans
- Brown Butter Bourbon Pecan Pie, 164–165
- Fig Pecan Jam with Port, 203
- French Silk Pie, 185
- German Chocolate Cupcakes, 160–161
- Quinoa Salad, 113

pecorino cheese, 35
pepitas, 213. See also pumpkin seeds
pepperoncini peppers, 103
peppers. See also chilies
- Aleppo, 218–219
- bell, 112, 215, 216
- habanero, 215
- jalapeno (See jalapeno peppers)
- pepperoncini, 103
- poblano, 76–77, 223
- red, in Risotto, 141
- yellow, 103

pickles
- Bread & Butter Pickles, 211
- Fresh Garlic Dill Pickles, 214

pie crusts, 159, 167
pie crusts, double, 80, 85, 164
pies
- Brown Butter Bourbon Pecan Pie, 164–165
- Chicken Pot Pie, 85–87
- Custard Pie, 166–167
- French Silk Pie, 185
- Kale and Sausage Pie, 80–81
- Nectarine Pie, 158–159
- Spiced Pear Custard Brulé Pie, 180–182

Pineapple Jalapeno Jelly, 216
pistachio nuts, 18
Pizza Crust and Pizza, 78–79
poblano peppers
- Green Chicken Enchiladas, 76–77
- White Chicken Chili, 223

pork, 84, 142, 48–49. See also bacon; sausage
port, 203
Post Chuck E. Cheese Recovery Salad, 110–111
potato chips, 173
potatoes
- Beef Burgundy, 151–152
- Chicken Bouillabaisse with Rouille, 148–149
- Chicken Pot Pie, 85–87
- French Fries, 101
- French Potato Salad, 146
- Moroccan Chickpea Stew, 220–221
- New Mexico Green Chili Stew with Chicken, 93
- Ribollita - Tuscan White Bean and Vegetable Stew, 56–57
- White Chicken Chili, 223

potato salad, French, 146
pot pie, 85–87
Pots de Crème (gluten free), 179
Pregnancy Salad, a.k.a. Hot Summer Night Tuna Salad, 114
prosciutto, 142
protein powder
- Green Smoothie, 95
- Warm & Satisfying Eggnog, 33

pumpkin bars, Keto, 190
pumpkin seeds
- Breakfast Cupcakes, 29
- California Slaw, 107
- Granola, 18
- Tuna Fish with Pickled Red Onions & Pepitas, 213

Q

Quiche Lorraine, 134–135
Quinoa Salad, 113

R

rabe, 52

radishes, 107
raisins, 142
raspberries, 26
Ratatouille, 103
reishi mushrooms, 217
Ribollita - Tuscan White Bean and Vegetable Stew, 56–57
ribs, 129
rice, 139–143
rice noodles, 83
ricotta cheese, 80–81
risi bisi-style risotto, 141
Risotto, 139–143
Roasted Asparagus with Soft Cooked Eggs, 35
Roasted Cauliflower, 102
Roasted Fall Vegetables, 90–91

S

salads
- Celery Apple Salad, 117
- Composed Niçoise Salad, 146–147
- Panzanella, 112
- Post Chuck E. Cheese Recovery Salad, 110–111
- Pregnancy Salad, a.k.a. Hot Summer Night Tuna Salad, 114
- Quinoa Salad, 113

salami, 48–49
salsa verde, 223
Salted Caramel, 170–171
Salted Chocolate Chip Cookies (gluten-free, vegan), 173
Salted Whiskey Caramel, 194
saltine crackers, 174–175
sauces
- Artichoke Dipping Sauce, 144
- Bolognese Sauce, 48–49
- bordelaise, 127
- Enchilada Sauce, 74
- Even Better, BEST Spaghetti Sauce, 46
- green enchilada, 76–77
- Oven Roasted Spaghetti Sauce, 43
- for pad thai, 83
- Peach Bourbon Barbecue Sauce, 218–219
- rouille, 149
- Salted Caramel, 170–171
- Sicilian Spaghetti Sauce, 45
- Spinach Bechamel, 49
- White Wine Butter Sauce, 64–65

sauerkraut, 84
sausage
- Kale and Sausage Pie, 80–81
- in Risotto, 140, 142

scones, 31
sherry
- Chicken and Dumplings, 68–69
- Chicken Pot Pie, 85–87
- Cream of Tomato Soup, 89

shopping tips, 10–12
Short Ribs, 129
shrimp
- Award-winning Shrimp Pad Thai, 83
- in Risotto, 140

Sicilian Spaghetti Sauce, 45
Skirt Steak, 73
slaw
- California Slaw, 107
- Sriracha Slaw, 70–71

Slow Cooker Turkey Breast, 82
smoothies, 95
snails, 138
sopressata, 48–49
soups
- Bone Broth, 202
- Broccoli Cheese Soup, 118
- Butternut Squash & Roasted Fall Vegetable Soup, 90–91
- Chicken Bouillabaisse with Rouille, 148–149
- Cream of Tomato Soup, 89
- Garlic Soup, 106

spaghetti sauces. See sauces
Spiced Pear Custard Brulé Pie, 180–182
Spicy Pickled Green Beans, 210
spinach
- Green Smoothie, 95
- Moroccan Chickpea Stew, 220–221
- in Risotto, 141
- Spinach Bechamel, 49

Spinach Bechamel, 49
squash
- Butternut Squash & Roasted Fall Vegetable Soup, 90–91
- Chicken Pot Pie, 85–87
- Even Better, BEST Spaghetti Sauce, 46
- in Risotto, 140

Sriracha sauce, 70–71
steak
- Filet Mignon with Bordelaise, 127
- Skirt Steak, 73

stews
- Moroccan Chickpea Stew, 220–221
- New Mexico Green Chili Stew with Chicken, 93
- Oysters Adrienne, 137
- Ribollita - Tuscan White Bean and Vegetable Stew, 56–57

stinging nettles, 217
strawberries, 26
Super Elderberry Syrup, 217
super-greens powder, 95
sweet potatoes
- Kale and Sausage Pie, 80–81
- Moroccan Chickpea Stew, 220–221

Swiss chard
- Green Smoothie, 95
- Moroccan Chickpea Stew, 220–221
- Ribollita - Tuscan White Bean and Vegetable

Stew, 56-57
syrup, elderberry, 217

T

tacos, 70-71
Tangy Mustard Vinaigrette, 111, 146
tapioca, 158-159, 180-182
Thanksgiving-style risotto, 141
toffee, 174-175
tomatoes
- Award-winning Shrimp Pad Thai, 83
- Bolognese Sauce, 48-49
- Chicken Bouillabaisse with Rouille, 148-149
- Composed Niçoise Salad, 146-147
- Cream of Tomato Soup, 89
- Even Better, BEST Spaghetti Sauce, 46
- Farmstand Guacamole, 209
- Moroccan Chickpea Stew, 220-221
- Oven Roasted Spaghetti Sauce, 43
- Panzanella, 112
- Peach Bourbon Barbecue Sauce, 218-219
- Ratatouille, 103
- Ribollita - Tuscan White Bean and Vegetable Stew, 56-57
- Sicilian Spaghetti Sauce, 45

tuna, canned
- Composed Niçoise Salad, 146-147
- Pregnancy Salad, a.k.a. Hot Summer Night Tuna Salad, 114
- Tuna Fish with Pickled Red Onions & Pepitas, 213

Tuna Fish with Pickled Red Onions & Pepitas, 213
turkey
- Bolognese Sauce, 48-49
- Slow Cooker Turkey Breast, 82

turnips, 151-152

U

Urfa biber chile, 218-219

V

Vacation Chicken, 66-67
vanilla extract, homemade, 204-206
veal, 125
vegetable dishes. See also salads
- Artichokes, 144
- Balsamic Onions, 212
- Broccoli Cheese Soup, 118
- Butternut Squash & Roasted Fall Vegetables Soup, 90-91
- California Slaw, 107
- Carrot Puree, 105
- Green Smoothie, 95
- Ratatouille, 103
- Roasted Asparagus with Soft Cooked Eggs, 35
- Roasted Cauliflower, 102
- Spicy Pickled Green Beans, 210

vermouth
- French Potato Salad, 146
- New Mexico Green Chili Stew with Chicken, 93

vinaigrettes. See also dressings
- Tangy Mustard Vinaigrette, 111, 146
- Vinaigrette, 109

vodka, 204-206

W

Warm & Satisfying Eggnog, 33
whiskey, 193-195. See also bourbon
white beans, 223
White Chicken Chili, 223
wine, red
- Beef Burgundy, 151-152
- Even Better, BEST Spaghetti Sauce, 46
- Filet Mignon with Bordelaise, 127
- Sicilian Spaghetti Sauce, 45

wine, white
- Bolognese Sauce, 48-49
- Chicken Bouillabaisse with Rouille, 148-149
- Chicken Tenderloins with White Wine Butter Sauce, 64-65
- Choucroute Garnie, 84
- Crab Omelet, 132-133
- Escargot, 138
- Osso Buco, 125
- Oysters Adrienne, 137
- Risotto, 139-143
- Vacation Chicken, 66-67

Z

zucchini
- Chicken Pot Pie, 85-87
- Even Better, BEST Spaghetti Sauce, 46
- Ratatouille, 103
- Zucchini Bread Cupcakes, 23

Zucchini Bread Cupcakes, 23

Acknowledgements

This creation from the heart would not have been possible without the help and support from one very fabulous babe.

STEPHANIE WASHBURN

Thank you for your editorial genius and for all of the love, dedication and commitment you offered to me and this book. You are love itself.

Thank You

... for your support, dedication, commitment and love! You all made this book possible.

Noah Ayon

Linda Bacelis-Bush
Kim Battista
Mallory Bryson
Dennis Conley
Laura Crowe

Nafis Fuad Didar
Cynthia Ellington
Lexi Ellis

Carol Evatt
Nim Evatt
Philip Evatt
Sue Evatt
Marie Green

Jennifer Hackman
Mas and Helge Jacobsen
Sarah Kerr
Maayke Mannaert
Melina Massetti
Katy McGuire
Sumiko Miles
Joyce Mojher
Joan Mollohan

Molly Nellman
Wendy Newell
Amy Peabody

Cara Pohle
Pam Rentz
Tonya Rine
Maham Safdar

Lauren Sims
Karen Smith
Mary Timmons-Schneider
Cori Tomlin
Katie Tsao

Susan Webb

Liz Wachsler
Jen Weers
Augustina Wilkins

Halley Yankanich
Hadley Zay
Olive Zay
Piper Zay
Steven Zay

Letter FROM THE AUTHOR

My name is Adrienne Evatt. I'm a mother to girls, a sister to brothers, a daughter, a wife, a baker and chef, a business coach and author, a Pilates and rowing enthusiast, a network marketing business owner, and a total gardening nerd. I'm also the owner of a farm, culinary business and farmstand. I've lived all over the world, and I love to cook.

I believe there is joy in cooking, just as there is joy in living life. This cookbook reflects that joy. Inside you'll find many of the recipes I use at our farmstand, as well as a healthy collection of recipes I enjoy making for loved ones, friends and family. Some of these I have gathered from my travels, others I created to perfection in my home kitchen.

There is something inside these pages for everyone! From time and budget friendly home cooked meals to restaurant quality fancy foods. Anyone can learn to make my recipes! If cooking is your favorite way to gather loved ones around the kitchen, like it is mine, then this is the book for you. This book was a labor of love over 35 years, and it comes directly from my heart.

Cooking is how I love people. I put my energy and good intentions into my special recipes. Each and every one is a favorite! I hope you enjoy my efforts. Happy cooking!

Xo, Adrienne

The Story

My story starts in California in the 1960's. My parents, Carol Rine Evatt (Carol) and Randall Nim Evatt (Nim) were both educated, intelligent, conservative, budget conscious, hard working people. They loved to play tennis, entertain, play bridge, and ski, and my brother Philip and I have countless memories of spending time as a family with other families with kids we were close to.

When I was born, my parents, especially my dad, was shocked to discover that I was a girl. He didn't think he made girls and it never crossed his mind that he should prepare for the possibility. So instead of being named Jack Evatt, after my grandfather, I remained nameless for a full week before they settled on Adrienne Lee Evatt as my name.

My childhood was magical, really. We had a big flowering magnolia tree in our front yard, and a navel orange tree as well. In the back was a giant Bing cherry tree that we had to climb to pick the cherries each year, and we would get dozens of paper grocery bags full and give them away to as many friends and neighbors that would accept them. We also had a sandbox, swings, and a walnut tree. One year when Philip was playing in the backyard he found an Indian arrowhead in the backyard. Many of the years we lived in California we had so many families for Thanksgiving that the kids table had to be outside because we wouldn't fit in the house all at once. Dad cooked the turkey, which had chunks of salt pork tied all over the outside of the bird, on the grill rotisserie in the backyard. I have memories of playing with other kids all day and seeing the adults laughing and having fun too.

Sunday mornings, Dad would wash his car (sometimes we helped), and then we would go get a donut. Most Sundays we also went to church with Mom. We lived in a part of California that is now referred to as Silicon Valley, but I like to joke that I lived there before it was cool, because it had no such name at the time. When Philip and I were in elementary school, we would walk to school from home and walk back home. Some days, we would stop and suck the sweet sap from the honeysuckle flowers on our way. Many days for fun, we rode our bikes.

When my dad got one of many job transfers and promotions, we moved (the 4th of 10 moves we made as a family before I turned 17) across the country to the Northeast (first Connecticut, followed by New York, New Jersey and Pennsylvania).

Each time we moved; we started over... all of us. New schools, new jobs, new friends, new clubs. Everyone worked hard and when we were together as a family, the happiest memories were the ones where we were dining out, cooking, or celebrating with a meal. And frankly, that was everything. Always being in a new place put pressure on us as individuals, and so family time was sacred. We didn't go on vacations or take trips much. Dinners and family time around the table were highly valuable.

Philip and I did sports. He was (and still is) an incredibly talented tennis player. He played soccer too, and was always at the center of the fun with friends. I was a competitive swimmer, a gymnast, artist, and dedicated reader and student. After high school, I headed to college in Virginia and Philip joined the military. We both ended up back home a few years later. He had finished his military commitment and I switched gears by taking a year off halfway through my University career. The truth is, I was practically failing and very unhappy. I never felt like I fit in at that school, and ultimately it was the best thing I ever did when I left. I got a job in a bank as a teller and supplemented my income with waitressing and bartending.

When I got an opportunity to attend our local Ivy League university, The University of Pennsylvania, as a summer school student without having to go through the entire application process, I leapt at the chance. I chose the most difficult class I could find in the hopes that it would make the admissions department take me seriously, Calculus. I aced it, and the college allowed me another class in the fall. They didn't allow me to matriculate. That would have required a full application, and my grades from my other school were horrendous. So, I gratefully accepted the opportunity to take one more class, paying for it with my tips from bartending. After another A+, I did that again, and again, and again. Once class at a time, paying with my tips, getting one A+ at a time. After 5 semesters and a 4.0 GPA, the University of Pennsylvania allowed me to matriculate. I continued taking classes, 1 or 2 at a time, paying with tips, until I completed my education.

After almost failing out of college in Virginia, I graduated with an Ivy League degree in Pennsylvania with honors, magna cum laude. I was never prouder of the hard work I dedicated, the long hours of study and late-night shifts. My parents were incredibly proud and instead of bartending tips paying for my last 2 classes, my parents offered to cover the cost for those. The best part of the gift was that the classes were in Italy. So I excitedly boarded a plane and spent my last summer of college in Florence, Italy, and my life was never the same.

Immersing myself in Italian culture was such a gift and was the precursor to a lifetime of travel. I had always had a deep DEEP desire to see other countries, especially France and Italy. Years later, I ended up living in Italy and that trip was the first of 33 (to date) to Florence. My love of food and entertaining was magnified on that trip. I felt understood there. I was with my people. I spoke Italian (not incredibly well, but well enough to be understood), had Italian friends, ate, drank, traveled and studied (in that order). I sobbed uncontrollably when I had to return home. I felt like it was going to be forever. One season passed and I started my 24-year career at a Fortune 5 company.

Incredibly, my company purchased an Italian utility, headquartered in Florence Italy mere months after my start date. Less than one year after my first visit there, I was back FOR WORK. They needed corporate finance trainees who spoke the language for the first physical inventory at Nuovo Pignone, and I fit the bill. I could not believe my luck.

My career continued for 24 years, and I continued to be pulled into assignments and positions that took me all over the world. It was a dream come true. I worked hard, sometimes to the brink of exhaustion and loved growing and developing as a corporate leader. I was referred to as a 'red hot'. I got big promotions, good raises, stock options and cool business trips. I met big wigs and went to the corporate training center many times to be groomed for bigger and bigger roles. I was given special projects by corporate officers who only wanted me to do the work. They would say things like (we need Evatt on this one). I also firmly believed in multiple income streams and was always trying different side hustles once I was firmly planted back in the United States. I had a cooking school that I ran from my home, and taught Pilates on the side both in a rented space (in a local church basement) as my own business and at a fancy gym. I bartended for friends who opened bars and needed support in their first months. I started this book.

I also wistfully dreamed of putting down roots. I had stopped counting how many times I moved when I hit 23 times. I have moved at least a dozen more times, but like I said, I stopped counting. I dreamed of getting back to California to live and putting roots down there. I would play the song "California Dreamin" by the Mamas and the Papas on cold winter days and sing and cry and wonder how I could make a corporate move that would get me there. Seventeen years into my career (and also thanks to a masters degree I earned over 3 years in the evenings when I was in my 10th year), I was transferred to Los Angeles. It was a lateral career move, and not particularly good for my career, but I didn't care. The move also almost bankrupt me when I had difficulties selling my house in Connecticut. It was probably the most stressful time of my life. While struggling with the financial side of things, I was also getting accustomed to a new job, new lifestyle and helping my dog recover after he was mishandled by the airline. It was a rocky start in California for sure.

Philip had also been transferred to Los Angeles a few years before with his company, and we had a magical few years drinking Jamba Juice and eating Wahoo Fish Tacos before each meeting our spouses, getting married and having children. He had three boys and I had three girls. Isn't that funny?

While pregnant with my second child, I started Urban Dreamer. My husband (Steven) and I had created a small urban farm in Los Angeles. I wanted to start another side hustle: a blog. So, I wrote some posts about cooking, gardening and homesteading on an urban farm, and that's when it began. I thought for months about what to call it before landing on the name. People would come over to buy fresh eggs from our chickens, or my homemade fig pecan jam with port, or canned spaghetti sauce.

Steven was doing the lion's share of the child rearing at that point. I was traveling for work again, so he generously became a stay-at-home dad to bear the brunt of the home duties. On the weekends, Steven and I would make elaborate plans to 'someday' move to Napa Valley with the kids and have our own vineyard. We would take trips when the budget allowed and soak in the countryside, the wine, the food, and the aura of the area. We became attached to the idea and loved talking about 'someday' when we would make the move. The kids would be able to enjoy the outdoors more, Steven would get a tractor, I would bake bread, and we would laugh and sing and drink wine and all would be lovely.

During 2 years of taking trips and getting to know the areas of Napa, Sonoma and Placer counties, we heard news that a large technology company was bringing 4000 jobs to our little area of Los Angeles. Our home value shot up 40%, and our move was instantly accelerated. My corporate job required proximity to a major airport only, so we put our house on the market, and after a couple of false starts with buyers, we made the move (10 years early) to a 20 acre property in Auburn, California.

I continued to travel for work while we set up house, planted crops, cleared defensible space to prepare for our first fire season, built a coop for our chickens, and got the kids settled into a new pre-school. Within 6 months, I was home recovering from a mysterious illness, and within another 6 months I was diagnosed with a rare (hereditary) autoimmune disorder that ended my corporate career for good.

There we were, on a 20 acre property that had been empty for almost 2 years, and it had fallen into some disrepair. The kids were 1, 3, and 5 and my bonus daughter was 12. Our primary income was gone. And I was sick. For 2 years, my network marketing company (premium skincare) kept us afloat. When I was feeling well enough, I worked to grow that business, and Steven went to truck driving school to get his class A license. He got a job as a truck driver for a local company. For the first time ever, I got to be the one to take the kids to and from school, go to parent teacher meetings, and shuttle them to activities. It was glorious!

We built a coop for our chickens (we actually brought them with us from LA). Their coop and run together were larger than my first house in Los Angeles. Lucky chickens! We planted fruit trees and hops and gardens with the thought of selling produce to farmers markets and hops to local microbreweries. We fixed fences and irrigation lines. We replaced gutters and bought cows. We repaired the well, the septic and our irrigation pond while clearing rat infested overgrown juniper bushes and endless tangles of thorny wild blackberries intermingled with poison oak. We ate our own beef, eggs and produce, cooked bread and rice and beans and relied on the food bank to help feed the family. We adopted farm cats when we started seeing snakes, and they took care of the mice and rats. The snakes left to find food elsewhere. Irrigation lines failed, deer broke down fences and we lost a lot of hard work, fresh food and beautiful fruit trees. But we kept going.

Overall, we worked so hard and we still do. The early years on the farm were filled with uncertainty and struggle, so the work tended to feel so heavy. There were months that we couldn't pay our bills, and we fed the family with donated food. A couple of years in, we started a farmstand at the bottom of our driveway. We offered some homegrown produce and eggs, jams and jellies, plant starts, granola and muffins. A handful of people stopped and shopped, and we decided to try it again the following week. My baked goods were the most popular, so I kept growing that part of the farmstand, and showing up every week. The farmstand became my thing and Steven worked the farm and drove for the trucking company.

This continued and eventually Steven started his own business using a water truck to drive as a contract firefighter for the state during fire season. My farmstand continued to grow until it became our main livelihood. What a blessing it has been to welcome our local community to our property. I love that it has become a place where people meet new friends and run into old friends that they haven't seen since high school or earlier. The farmstand is commonly referred to in my earshot (happily) as a hidden gem. Isn't that cool? Urbandreamerfarm.org

During the many years of growing the farmstand, my corporate brain started to get restless. I desperately wanted to find an outlet to help people using my vast corporate experiences, long list of certifications and multitude of life and business experiences.

When I discovered life coaching the first time, it did not seem like a fit to me. But once I came across a more helpful coach myself, she helped me tremendously and I felt like I had discovered the secret of the universe. I could not wait to help others. My business and life coaching business is SUCH a joy for me and the feeling of helping others change their lives and businesses is indescribable. AdrienneEvatt.com

I am incredibly humbled by my success and so grateful for my supporters, customers, fans and friends who have been there over the years. My whole journey has been decorated by the incredible people who have been there for me along the way.

Dedication

This book would not exist without the love of food inspired by my dad, Nim Evatt. My father's mentality of "try everything at least once" was the cornerstone of my upbringing as it related to food. He taught me to experiment with cooking and baking until the results were nothing short of phenomenal. One of his favorite expressions was "you broke the code on this", meant to indicate he could not imagine it being any better.

When I was 17, I made a pasta sauce with fresh tomatoes, repeatedly, for a period of many months until the whole family loved it. The sauce had chopped tomatoes, onions, crushed red pepper and butter and it clung to the pasta and had so much flavor. It was probably one of the first sauces that I was proud of. My love of food and love of cooking and willingness to experiment to make something better came from my dad.

I love and miss him deeply. I know he is looking down on me with all his favorite foods and the memories and feelings they create.

I dedicate this book to you, Dad.

ALSO BY
Adrienne Evatt

- Life Skills for Teens
- The Extraordinary Planner - ORIGINAL
- Life Design Workbook for Business Owners
- Kale is a Four Letter Word (contributor)
- Coming soon: Financial Literacy for Young Adults

Your Review

Now you have everything you need to enhance your own cooking skills and repertoire, it's time to pass on your newfound knowledge and show other readers where they can find the same help.

Simply by leaving your honest opinion of this book on Amazon, you'll show other cooks and lovers of comfort foods where they can find the information they're looking for and pass their passion for food forward.

Thank you for your help. The skills are kept alive when we pass on our knowledge – and you're helping me to do just that.

CLICK HERE
TO LEAVE
YOUR REVIEW.

OTHER WAYS YOU CAN HELP

TELL SOMEONE ABOUT
THIS BOOK

LEAVE A FABULOUS
REVIEW

GIFT THIS BOOK TO
SOMEONE

DONATE THE BOOK TO
A CHARITY AUCTION
OR OTHER CAUSE

PS - Fun fact:

If you provide something of value to another person, it makes you more valuable to them. If you'd like goodwill straight from another - and you believe this book will help them - send this book their way.

Made in the USA
Las Vegas, NV
22 February 2025

18535661R00148